PRAISE FOR
THE THEORY OF MAGNUS OVEA

The Theory of Magnus Ovea seamlessly integrates rigorous analysis with practical application, offering a comprehensive framework that mirrors the precision and resilience essential in cybersecurity. The theory transcends traditional boundaries, providing insights into human potential. When applied to cybersecurity, these insights help us understand and influence human behavior, ultimately enhancing security measures and optimizing performance in an increasingly complex world.

GITI JAVIDI, PH.D.
Professor and Director of Information Assurance
& Cyber Security Management, University of South Florida

As Kurt Lewin famously remarked, "There is nothing so practical as a good theory." The MAGNUS OVEA Theory offers a pan-theoretical explication that brings together the work of theorists Albert Bandura, Victor Vroom, and Daniel Siegel into a practical, cohesive framework for fulfilling one's potential. Underlying the theories of Bandura, Vroom, and Siegel is the meta-philosophy and tradition of Bushido, as illuminated by Miyamoto Musashi in *The Book of Five Rings*.

Read through this lens, it becomes apparent that MAGNUS OVEA is ultimately a book about Warriorship. In this context, a "warrior" is defined outside the limited concept of those who engage in combat operations. A "warrior" is an individual who makes personal sacrifices in the service of values that he or she holds as sacred, someone who, as authors Javidi and Ellis state, "steers [one's] course with intentionality and purpose" and aims to master their self by "transcending the narrow confines of self-interest." For warriors, hardships and not merely to be endured but are the crucible through which oneself and one's community develop in complex but synchronous inter-dependence.

In *The Theory of Magnus Ovea*, Javidi and Ellis provide a meta-framework—the "11 Rings" for developing and deploying the qualities of warriorship in a range of domains, including family units (As they say, "Family is not just a unit. It's a sanctuary of love, understanding and growth, where each member plays a vital role in shaping a shared journey of happiness and fulfillment"), professional endeavors, close relationships, financial health, and physical health optimization. Thus, MAGNUS OVEA takes the reader from theory to practice, engaging us with a series of specific, actionable habits to cultivate warriorship and fulfill our potential.

SHAUNA 'DOC' SPRINGER, PH.D.

In terms of human performance and well-being, economics have failed to take into consideration the interconnectivity and interdependencies of human life, and thereby, economists have been unable to find solutions for marginalized communities. Alas! The guidance provided by a must-read new theory—*The Theory of Magnus Ovea*—by Mitch Javidi and Brian Ellis explains the power of thinking about such interconnectivities.

LYNN ILON, PH.D.

Professor Emeritus, Seoul National University (SNU), Seoul, South Korea

Mitch Javid and Brian Ellis offer readers multiple ways of navigating family, work, leadership, learning challenges and opportunities at a time when societies face complex, new, and longstanding pressures. Crucially, *The Theory of Magnus Ovea* is anchored to nurturing and supporting individual, relational awareness, and prosperity while employing compelling theoretical and practical insights to astutely unveil ways of enhancing human performance and well-being.

PAM BISHOP, PH.D.

Western University, Ontario, Canada

The MAGNUS OVEA Theory presents an insightful and transformative framework for understanding human performance, potential, and purpose. Dr. Javidi and Mr. Ellis delve deeply into the intricacies of human behavior, offering profound and fresh perspectives that illuminate the path to self-improvement and collective success. By identifying the key obstacles that hinder our progress and proposing actionable strategies for advancement, this book serves as a comprehensive guide for anyone seeking to unlock their full potential.

Whether you're striving for personal growth, leading a team, or aiming to enhance organizational effectiveness, the MAGNUS OVEA Theory provides the tools and insights necessary to achieve your goals. This book is not just a read, but a journey toward a more fulfilled and effective life. Embrace the opportunity to transform yourself and those around you with the wisdom and guidance found within these pages.

KEN KEIS, PH.D.

Bestselling author of *Why Aren't You More Like Me?*

THE THEORY OF
MAGNUS
OVEA

THE THEORY OF
MAGNUS
OVEA

A GENERAL THEORY OF HUMAN PERFORMANCE & WELLBEING

MITCH JAVIDI, PH.D.
WITH BRIAN ELLIS

THE THEORY OF MAGNUS OVEA
A GENERAL THEORY OF HUMAN PERFORMANCE & WELLBEING

BY MITCH JAVIDI, PH.D., WITH BRIAN ELLIS

Published by the Readiness Network Publishing., Holly Springs, NC.

Readiness Network Publishing
338 Raleigh Street,
Holly Springs, NC 27540.

For general information or to obtain academic review copies, don't hesitate to contact Readiness Network Publishing at 338 Raleigh Street, Holly Springs, NC 27540.

Readiness Network Publishing produces books in various print and electronic formats. Some content that appears in print may not be available in electronic books and vice versa.

Library of Congress Cataloging-in-Publications Data
Name: Mitch Javidi, Ph.D. with Brian Ellis
Title: The Theory of MAGNUS OVEA:
A General Theory of Human Performance and Wellbeing

Editorial Review: Sam Spiegel
Forward: Anthony Normore, Ph.D
Interior and Cover Designer: PearCreative.ca
Image Graphics: Muhammad Sujon

ISBN: Print 978-1-7377855-3-8

This book is dedicated to the trailblazers in human behavior and performance—those who tirelessly chase the boundaries of human potential. Your pioneering spirit fuels our commitment to inspire, contribute, learn, and share the insights that drive us forward. Thank you for setting the path for us to walk together and elevating our GREAT to MAGNUS.

CONTENTS

FOREWORD

In *The Theory of MAGNUS OVEA: A General Theory of Human Performance & Well-Being*, authors Mitch Javidi and Brian Ellis propose a groundbreaking paradigm poised to revolutionize our understanding of human performance and well-being. The theory transcends traditional boundaries, offering actionable, teachable, and quantifiable insights into the expansive realm of human potential. At its core, the MAGNUS OVEA Theory is a theory of theories. A theory is a rational type of abstract thinking about a phenomenon—in this case MAGNUS OVEA—or the results of such thinking. A theory can be a body of knowledge which may or may not be associated with any specific explanatory models. To theorize is to develop this body of knowledge. As an everyday word, theory is simply "looking at, viewing, beholding", but in more technical contexts it refers to contemplative or speculative understandings of ideas and hunches such as those of philosophers, as opposed to more practical ways of knowing things, like that of skilled orators or artisans[1].

Theory is often distinguished from practice or praxis. The question of whether theoretical models of work are relevant to work itself is of interest to scholars of professions that range from anthropology, medicine, engineering, law, economics, politics, and management to

1

education, film, humanities, music, physics, philosophy, psychology, sociology, and architecture—to name a few.

Through the lens of MAGNUS OVEA, Javidi and Ellis help the reader navigate the 11 Rings of Performance, encompassing diverse aspects of mastery to operationalize the theory of theories. The theory-theory is a scientific theory relating to the human development of understanding about the outside world. It asserts that individuals hold a basic theory of psychology to infer the mental states of others, such as their beliefs, desires, or emotions[2]. This information is used to understand the intentions behind that person's actions or predict future behavior. This approach has become popular with psychologists as it gives a basis from which to explore human social understanding, social learning theory, theory of mind, simulation theory, social cognitive theory, expectancy theory of motivation, path-goal theory, hierarchy of needs theory, science of attunement, and now MAGNUS OVEA Theory.

In MAGNUS OVEA Theory, human performance plays a pivotal role in understanding how it guides and evolves. From a general knowledge of human performance, we understand the various simple elements that form the foundation for sustainable human performance including mindset, nutrition, movement, and recovery[3]. These components are simple, yet universal. They are essential at a minimum for survival. Moreover, to sustain performance requires balance in several critical interlinked areas of well-being—physical, mental, emotional, economic, and spiritual; it requires a willingness to adapt to change and to make difficult choices, as well as communicate those choices through an authentic display of self-expression that creates value for others. Well-being plays a central role in ethics since what a person ought to do depends, at least to some degree, on what would make someone's life get better or worse[4].

Well-being is the central subject of positive psychology which aims to discover the factors that contribute to human well-being. MAGNUS OVEA theory suggests that these factors consist in having positive emotions, being engaged in an activity, having good relationships with other people, finding meaning in one's life and a sense of accomplishment in the pursuit of one's goals. The well-being of a person is what is good for the person. The causal network account holds that well-being is the product of many factors—feelings, beliefs, motivations, habits, resources, and so forth—that are causally related in ways that explain increases in well-being or ill-being[5]. The theory of MAGNUS OVEA and its affiliated rings of performance are concerned with reflection about what holds the greatest value in life—the factors that contribute the most to a well-lived and fulfilling life such as positive emotions, engagement, relationships, meaning and purpose, and accomplishments. The broad dimensions of well-being include the natural environment, personal well-being, our relationships, health, what we do, where we live, personal finance, the economy, education and skills, and governance.

Personal well-being is a particularly important dimension which we define as how satisfied we are with our lives, our sense that what we do in life is worthwhile, our day-to-day emotional experiences and our wider mental well-being in terms of experience and pursuit of excellence, health, happiness, and prosperity. It is something sought by just about everyone because it includes so many positive things—feeling happy, healthy, socially connected, and purposeful. To this end, it is incumbent upon us to understand how well-being occurs in our lives[6]. MAGNUS OVEA, through the presentation of 11 rings, demonstrates how the theory looks in practice by focusing on the various types pf well-being including: emotional well-being with focus on how to practice stress- management, relaxation techniques, be resilient, boost self-love, and generate the emotions that lead to good feelings; physical well-being—ability to improve the functioning of your body through healthy living and good lifestyle habits; social well-being which focuses on how to communicate, develop meaningful relationships with others, and maintain a support network that helps you overcome loneliness; workplace well-being that focuses on the ability to maintain a work-life balance, pursue interests, values, and life purpose in order to gain meaning, happiness, and enrichment professionally; and societal well-being which focuses on the ability to actively participate in a thriving community, culture, and environment.

The Theory of MAGNUS OVEA: A General Theory of Human Performance & Well-Being, acknowledges and reconfirms the complexity and transformative power of the human experience. Further, the proposed theory, along with the 11 rings of performance and its domains empower individuals to review, participate, adapt, and navigate with transcendence, spryness and dexterity while maximizing their chances of success in the options, directions, and opportunities in which they choose to undertake.

ANTHONY H. NORMORE, PH.D.

Professor Emeritus, California State University Dominguez Hills
President, National Command and Staff College

PREFACE

Have you ever stumbled upon something unexpectedly precious and life-changing?

Imagine a moment etched vividly in memory, as if it happened just yesterday.

It was June 26, 1973, around 5 p.m., when my father ushered me into the world of Martial Arts. At that moment, my heart was more dedicated to European football, or soccer as it is commonly known.

My father, silent but proud, accompanied me to the school while I reluctantly entered my first session, my face betraying anger and disappointment.

On our way home, my father handed me an old, weathered book. "I've held onto this book for many years, revisiting its pages countless times and sharing its wisdom with friends. I want to pass it on to you today, hoping you'll discover your unique path within its words," he shared.

With a knowing look, he continued, "I understand that martial arts might not be your immediate passion, but remember, 'you do not know what you do not know,' my son. This book may hold the secrets of self-defense, but it also conceals profound insights into human behavior and personal growth. In time, you'll come to appreciate it." He added, "I only ask that you approach this book patiently. I delve into it more deeply than ever and interpret it for self-defense, personal evolution, and overall success in life. We won't discuss the book, you and I, for what we each gain from it is a personal journey of discovery."

Without knowing how to respond, I said, "Thank you, Dad."

And so, *The Book of Five Rings*, penned by the legendary Japanese swordsman Miyamoto Musashi in the early 17th century, became a steadfast companion on my life's journey. I returned to it year after year, discovering it to be a timeless masterpiece that encompasses strategy, martial arts, profound philosophy, and the essence of human behavior.

Musashi's legacy as a warrior and philosopher infuses his work with a depth that transcends mere tactics. His book is divided into five parts, each symbolizing a crucial facet of strategy and offering insights that ripple through various aspects of life. Let's embark on a voyage through these parts, each a treasure trove of wisdom.

> **The first Ring, Earth (Chi no Maki):** Imagine this section as the solid ground beneath your feet, emphasizing the importance of mastering the basics. Musashi underscores the significance of proper posture, balance, and footwork—the foundational building blocks for all future endeavors.

> **The second Ring, Water (Sui no Maki):** This part likens itself to water's adaptability, teaching us to be flexible and responsive in the face of ever-changing circumstances. Just as water flows around obstacles, it urges us to value adaptability in navigating life's complexities.

> **The third Ring, Fire (Ka no Maki):** Symbolizing intensity, the fire section encourages an unwavering offensive or an "Intentional or

Deliberate" approach. Musashi advises swift, deliberate actions to overwhelm an opponent's strategy or efforts, akin to fire consuming everything in its path. One needs relentless determination and the ability to seize opportunities.

The fourth Ring, Wind (Fu no Maki): Wind, represents the subtlety of timing and distance. Musashi delves into understanding an opponent's intentions, recognizing their rhythm, and identifying the perfect moment to act. This part emphasizes the importance of being in tune with the flow of events mentally, emotionally, physically, and spiritually—a skill applicable not just in combat but also in negotiations, decision-making, and personal interactions.

The fifth Ring, Void (Ku no Maki): Musashi's teachings culminate in the concept of the void, where technique and strategy transcend limitations. This section explores the idea of "no-mindedness," advocating for mental clarity free of distractions and preconceptions with emotional fitness. It empowers us to act intuitively and effectively, harnessing the power of the present moment through resilience and capacity-building tools we encounter and develop.

For me, this book was a life-transforming revelation. I've pored over its pages more times than I can count and have shared its profound wisdom with audiences across the globe. Its relevance stretches far beyond its historical martial origins, offering deep insights applicable to various aspects of life, including personal development, peak performance, and resilience.

In our quest to better understand Musashi's wisdom, we are introducing our own *11 Rings of MAGNUS OVEA* in this book. Just as Musashi's timeless teachings transcend the realm of martial arts, our exploration of the 11 Rings of Peak Performance extends beyond the boundaries of traditional disciplines, guiding us toward unlocking our fullest potential. Like Musashi's legendary "Ring of Void," our journey knows no bounds, taking us into the depths of our potential to elevate "***GREAT to MAGNUS***."

> *"If you inspire yourself and those around you to answer the call of duty and obligation by going beyond to **dream more**, **learn more**, **do more**, and **become more** while building capacities **across 11 Rings of peak performance** for yourself, your family, your community, and our nation, you are **MAGNUS**."*

MITCH JAVIDI, PH.D.
Call Sign "MAGNUS"
April 23, 2024

PART I
FOUNDATION

"Theory serves as the intricate map that navigates us through the labyrinthine complexities of knowledge, illuminating the hidden pathways of understanding. The guiding compass charts our course, offering direction amidst the vast expanse of the unknown. In contrast, practice becomes the wind that fills our sails, propelling us forward on the voyage of discovery. The tangible force breathes life into our theoretical constructs, transforming abstract concepts into tangible realities. Together, theory and practice form an inseparable union, enriching the other as we journey ever closer to enlightenment."

CHAPTER 1
INTRODUCTION

In the vast landscape of human endeavor, amidst the ebb and flow of daily life, lies the pursuit of excellence—a quest to unlock the full spectrum of human potential and achieve unprecedented levels of performance and well-being.

Within this pursuit, this book introduces MAGNUS OVEA as a comprehensive theory guiding human performance and well-being.

Drawing from psychology, neuroscience, and organizational behavior, MAGNUS OVEA merges insights from Bandura, Vroom, and Siegel to offer practical strategies for achieving greatness. We explore Bandura's Social Cognitive Theory, Vroom's Expectancy Theory, and Siegel's Science of Attunement as foundational pillars. These theories illuminate the dynamics of behavior, motivation, and emotional regulation, providing a roadmap that inspires personal and professional growth.

Through the lens of MAGNUS OVEA, we navigate the 11 Rings of Performance, encompassing diverse aspects of mastery to operationalize the theory of theories. Within each ring, we unravel the Dynamic

Threads (DT) of life's tapestry, understanding the changing topography of each human's experience.

Our travel culminates in the GREAT to MAGNUS Journey, a pathway toward realizing our fullest potential. Along the way, we introduce the GREAT to MAGNUS Journey and our justification for why MAGNUS OVEA is a theory of theories. Furthermore, we recommend a path forward with strategies for future research. This includes inviting the scientific community to contact us for independent or joint studies using our formula for calculating the MAGNUS Index and associated instruments and diagnostics not included in this book edition.

Join us on this transformative journey as we uncover the keys to elevating our GREAT to MAGNUS, guided by the MAGNUS OVEA Theory.

INSPIRE—EDUCATE—IMPACT—TRANSCEND

CHAPTER 2

BANDURA'S SOCIAL COGNITIVE THEORY

Albert Bandura's Social Cognitive Theory is a cornerstone in psychology, illuminating the intricate relationship between individual cognition, behavior, and the social environment. This theory provides invaluable insights into the processes of learning and development, underscoring the significance of observation, imitation, and self-regulation.[7]

Bandura's Theory offers a comprehensive framework for understanding human behavior by integrating cognitive, behavioral, and environmental factors. Its emphasis on observational learning, self-efficacy, and reciprocal determinism has profound implications across various domains, from education and therapy to organizational behavior and societal change. By elucidating the intricate interplay between individual agency and social context, Bandura's theory continues to shape our understanding of human behavior and inform interventions to facilitate positive outcomes and personal growth.

In his theory, Bandura posited that individuals learn through direct experience and observing others. This process, known as observational learning or modeling, activates one to acquire new knowledge, skills, and behaviors by witnessing the actions and consequences of others.[8]

- **Self-Efficacy:** Central to Bandura's theory is the concept of self-efficacy, which refers to an individual's belief in their capability to execute specific actions to achieve desired outcomes successfully. Self-efficacy significantly influences individuals' engagement in activities, perseverance in facing challenges, and goal attainment.

- **Reciprocal Determinism:** Bandura proposed reciprocal determinism, highlighting the dynamic interaction between personal factors (such as cognition, emotions, and biological predispositions), environmental influences (including social, cultural, and situational factors), and behavior. This bidirectional relationship underscores how individuals and their environment continually shape and influence each other over time.[9]

- **Self-Regulation:** Social Cognitive Theory underscores the importance of self-regulation, wherein individuals actively monitor, evaluate, and adjust their thoughts, feelings, and behaviors to achieve desired outcomes. Self-regulation involves setting goals, planning strategies, monitoring progress, and making necessary adjustments.[10]

The Theory has proven diverse implications across various domains, including:

- **Education:** Understanding the role of observation and modeling informs teaching strategies that utilize peer modeling, demonstrations, and vicarious reinforcement to enhance learning outcomes. Additionally, fostering students' self-efficacy and self-regulatory skills promotes academic success and motivation.[11]

- **Psychology and Therapy:** Social Cognitive Theory has been instrumental in therapeutic interventions such as cognitive-behavioral therapy (CBT), which targets individuals' beliefs, attitudes, and self-regulatory processes to facilitate adaptive changes in behavior and cognition. [12]

- **Socialization and Development:** Bandura's theory illuminates the socialization process, emphasizing the influence of social modeling and reinforcement in shaping individuals' attitudes, values, and behaviors. Understanding these mechanisms is crucial for promoting prosocial behavior and preventing adverse outcomes such as aggression or substance abuse.[13]

- **Organizational Behavior:** Social Cognitive Theory informs our understanding of leadership, motivation, and organizational behavior. Cultivating a supportive environment enhances employees' self-efficacy and promotes effective modeling of desired behaviors.[14]

CHAPTER 3

BANDURA'S SOCIAL LEARNING THEORY

Social learning theory proposes that learning is not a solitary endeavor but a cognitive process deeply intertwined with social interactions. Rooted in keen observation and sometimes direct instruction, individuals assimilate behaviors, even without immediate reinforcement or the opportunity for direct replication. Through social learning, we understand how we learn by observing behaviors and deciphering the consequences—both rewarding and punitive—that others experience, a phenomenon known as vicarious reinforcement.[15]

The historical roots of social learning theory trace back to the mid-20th century when pioneers like B.F. Skinner[16] and Clark Leonard Hull[17] set the groundwork for understanding human behavior. Skinner's empirical approach to verbal behavior and Hull's exploration of stimulus-response theories provided foundational insights, setting the stage for the emergence of social learning theory. Julian B. Rotter's groundbreaking work further expanded upon these foundations, emphasizing the dynamic interplay between individuals and their environment.[18] At the same time, Abert Bandura's seminal studies on interpersonal learning experiences challenged traditional theories, leading to a holistic understanding of social learning as supported by Vroom in 1964.[19]

Bandura's contributions were pivotal in shaping our understanding of social learning. His Bobo doll experiments revealed the rapid acquisition of novel behaviors through social observation, challenging existing theories.[20] Bandura's theory, as defined in 1977, integrates behavioral and cognitive perspectives, emphasizing the cognitive processes inherent in social learning. It posits that learning occurs within a social context, involving observation, information extraction, and decision-making based on these observations. Reinforcement, while significant, does not solely dictate learning outcomes. Instead, the theory underscores the reciprocal influence of cognition, environment, and behavior, painting a dynamic portrait of the learning process.

Bandura's theory suggests that individuals learn through observation, imitation, and modeling. The formula proposed in theory can be summarized as follows:

- **Observation (O):** The first component of the formula is observation, which involves paying attention to the behavior of others in one's social environment. Individuals actively observe the actions, attitudes, and outcomes of others' behaviors.
- **Modeling (M):** The second component is modeling, where individuals emulate or imitate their observed behaviors. This involves replicating the actions of role models or peers they perceive as competent or influential.
- **Reinforcement (R):** The third component is reinforcement, which refers to the negative and positive aspects or

consequences of the behavior being observed and imitated. Reinforcement is crucial in determining whether the observed behavior will likely be repeated.

- **Expectations (E):** Another integral aspect of the formula is expectations, which are formed based on the outcomes observed in others' behavior. Individuals assess the likelihood of similar outcomes if they engage in the same behavior.

- **Motivation (M):** Lastly, motivation influences whether individuals choose to replicate observed behaviors. Motivation can be intrinsic, driven by internal desires or goals, or extrinsic, influenced by external rewards or punishments associated with the behavior.

The formula proposed in social learning theory suggests that individuals learn not only through direct experience but also by observing and modeling the behaviors of others. The interplay between observation, imitation, reinforcement, expectations, and motivation shapes the learning process, allowing individuals to acquire new behaviors and skills within their social context.

CHAPTER 4

VROOM'S EXPECTANCY THEORY

Victor Vroom's Expectancy Theory of Leadership is a seminal framework that explores the relationship between motivation, effort, and performance within organizational contexts.[21]

Developed in the 1960s, this theory provides insights into how leaders can effectively motivate their followers by understanding and manipulating key psychological variables. At its core, Vroom's theory suggests that individuals are encouraged to act in specific ways based on their beliefs about the relationship between effort, performance, and outcomes.

Central to Vroom's Expectancy Theory are three key components:

- **Expectancy:** This component refers to an individual's belief that their efforts will result in a desired level of performance. In other words, it assesses the perceived probability that exerting effort will lead to successful performance. Factors influencing expectancy include an individual's skills, experience, and the clarity of task instructions.

- **Instrumentality:** Instrumentality represents the belief that desired outcomes or rewards will follow successful performance. It focuses on the perceived connection between performance and outcomes. If individuals believe their efforts will be rewarded, they are more likely to be motivated to exert effort. Factors influencing instrumentality include trust in the reward system and the perceived fairness of reward distribution.

- **Valence:** Valence refers to the value or attractiveness of the outcomes or rewards associated with successful performance. It reflects the individual's personal preferences and goals. For example, one employee may value a monetary bonus, while another may prefer recognition or opportunities for career advancement. The higher the valence attached to an outcome, the more motivated an individual will be to achieve it.

Vroom proposed a formula as part of his Expectancy Theory. The formula, often referred to as Vroom's Expectancy Theory equation, is as follows:

$$\textbf{Motivation} = \text{Expectancy} \times \text{Instrumentality} \times \text{Valence}$$

In this equation:

- **Expectancy (E)** represents how strong the perceived relationship is between the individual's effort and performance of the behavior.[22]
- **Instrumentality (I)** represents how strong the perceived relationship is between performing a behavior and the desired outcome.

- **Valence (*V*)** represents how desirable (or undesirable) a particular outcome is to an individual.

The product of these three factors is the individual's motivation to engage in a particular behavior or task.

Vroom's equation illustrates that the presence of one factor does not solely determine motivation but is instead influenced by the interaction of multiple factors. Each factor—expectancy, instrumentality, and valence—plays a crucial role in shaping an individual's motivation levels and subsequent behavior within an organizational context. Leaders can utilize this equation to analyze and understand the motivational dynamics within their teams and identify areas where adjustments may be needed to enhance motivation and performance.

CHAPTER 5

INTERWOVEN THREADS: EXPLORING BANDURA AND VROOM'S THEORIES

Bandura's Social Cognitive Theory and Social Learning Theory share significant commonalities and interrelations with Vroom's Expectancy Theory despite originating from different psychological perspectives. Understanding these theories' intersections sheds light on the complex dynamics influencing human behavior and motivation within various contexts.

Both Bandura's Social Cognitive Theory and Social Learning Theory emphasize the role of observation, imitation, and modeling in learning. Individuals acquire new behaviors not only through direct experience but also by observing others' actions and their consequences. This notion aligns with Vroom's Expectancy Theory, which underscores individuals' beliefs about the outcomes of their actions. In all three theories, individuals' expectations are pivotal in shaping their behaviors and motivation.

Bandura's concept of self-efficacy, a central tenet of Social Cognitive Theory, parallels Vroom's expectancy component. Self-efficacy reflects individuals' beliefs in their ability to perform specific tasks and achieve desired outcomes. Similarly, expectancy in Vroom's theory represents individuals' belief that their efforts will lead to successful performance. Both self-efficacy and expectancy influence individuals' motivation levels and willingness to engage in tasks or behaviors.

Moreover, Bandura's reciprocal determinism highlights the dynamic interaction between personal factors, environmental influences, and behavior. This bidirectional relationship resonates with Vroom's theory, which acknowledges the impact of individuals' beliefs and perceptions about their environment, motivation, and behavior. In both theories, the environment significantly determines individuals' actions and outcomes, shaping their behavioral responses.

Furthermore, Bandura's emphasis on reinforcement and modeling in Social Learning Theory aligns with Vroom's concept of instrumentality. Both theories recognize the importance of perceived connections between actions, outcomes, and rewards in motivating individuals. Whether through vicarious reinforcement in social learning or the perceived link between performance and rewards in Expectancy Theory, individuals are encouraged by the anticipation of desirable outcomes.

While Bandura's theories focus more on cognitive and behavioral processes, and Vroom's theory centers on motivational dynamics within organizational contexts, they converge on the fundamental understanding of human behavior as influenced by mental, social, and environmental factors. By integrating these theories, we gain a holistic perspective on human motivation and behavior, applicable across diverse domains such as education, therapy, and organizational leadership.

In summary, Bandura's Social Cognitive Theory and Social Learning Theory, alongside Vroom's Expectancy Theory, offer complementary insights into the intricate interplay between cognition, behavior, motivation, and the social environment. Understanding the commonalities and relationships between these theories enriches our understanding of human behavior and provides a robust framework for addressing motivational challenges and fostering positive outcomes in various settings.

CHAPTER 6

SIEGEL'S SCIENCE OF ATTUNEMENT

Daniel Siegel, a psychiatrist and researcher renowned for his work in interpersonal neurobiology, delves into how our relationships and experiences mold the structure and function of our brains. Central to his discourse is the mind-brain relationship and the notion of "attunement."[23]

Siegel posits that the mind transcends the confines of the brain, emerging from the intricate interplay among the brain, body, and environment. He conceptualizes the "mind" as an embodied and relational process where mental phenomena arise from integrating neural activity, bodily sensations, and interpersonal encounters.[24]

According to Siegel, attunement is a cornerstone of healthy relationships and optimal brain development. It denotes the capacity to synchronize emotionally and psychologically with others, grasping and resonating with their internal states. Attunement entails qualities like empathy, emotional regulation, and interpersonal connection. Siegel advocates for its pivotal role in sculpting the developing brain and fostering emotional well-being.[25] To visualize Dr. Siegel's attunement, we offer the following illustration as we have interpreted it.

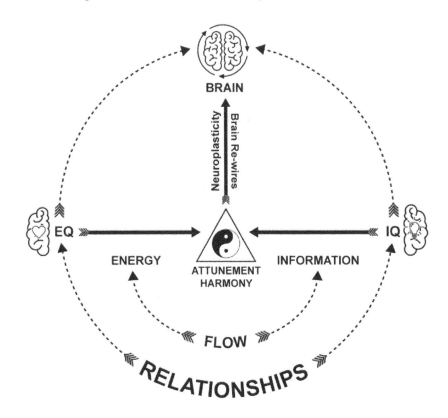

Daniel Siegel views the mind as an emergent product of brain-body-environment interactions. He underscores the significance of attuned relationships in fostering robust brain development and psychological well-being, highlighting the prefrontal cortex's (PFC) nine functions.[26] Nestled behind our foreheads, the PFC orchestrates a suite of cognitive functions vital to our daily functioning.[27]

BODY REGULATION: THE SENTINEL WITHIN

The prefrontal cortex is responsible for vigilantly monitoring our body's vital signs. Like a diligent sentinel, it monitors our heart rate, breathing patterns, and other physiological markers, ensuring a harmonious balance. This innate automated system is the foundation of our physical health, enabling us to adapt to life's challenges and maintain our well-being with strength and resilience.[28]

ATTUNED COMMUNICATION: THE LANGUAGE OF CONNECTION

Effective communication reigns supreme in the intricate tapestry of human relationships. With its exquisite sensitivity to emotional nuances, the prefrontal cortex is pivotal in fostering genuine connection and understanding. Through attuned communication, we transcend the barriers of words, resonating with others on a deeper, more profound level. In these moments of genuine connection, the true essence of our humanity unfolds, binding us together in shared experiences and emotions.[29]

EMOTIONAL BALANCE: NAVIGATING THE INNER STORM

Life is a tumultuous journey, replete with highs and lows, triumphs, and tribulations. Amidst this ever-changing landscape, the prefrontal cortex acts as our steadfast rudder, guiding our course through the storm of our emotions with unwavering poise. Maintaining a delicate equilibrium amidst the tumultuous currents of our inner world shields us from despair and the pitfalls of impulsivity, allowing us to weather the storms of life with resilience and grace.[30]

RESPONSE FLEXIBILITY: THE ART OF DELIBERATE ACTION

In the heat of the moment, our instincts often clamor for control, urging us to react impulsively to the challenges that confront us. Yet, true freedom lies in the space between stimulus and response. With its remarkable capacity for response flexibility, the prefrontal cortex empowers us to pause, reflect, and choose our actions thoughtfully. In this sacred pause, we harness the power of deliberate action, steering our course with intentionality and purpose.[31]

EMPATHY: THE BRIDGE OF UNDERSTANDING

At the heart of human connection lies empathy—the ability to recognize, understand, and resonate with the emotions of others. Guided by the compassionate embrace of the prefrontal cortex, we transcend the boundaries of self and others, forging deep and meaningful connections built on mutual understanding and respect. Differences dissolve in the empathic space we create, and unity prevails, illuminating the path toward a more compassionate and inclusive world.[32]

INSIGHT: ILLUMINATING THE PATH WITHIN

In the labyrinthine depths of the human psyche, insight serves as our guiding light, illuminating the hidden recesses of our inner world. Through mindful awareness and introspection, facilitated by the prefrontal cortex, we unravel the tangled threads of our personal history, discern the patterns that shape our present circumstances, and envision the possibilities on the horizon. In the sanctuary of self-reflection, we embark on a journey of self-discovery, reclaiming our agency and charting our path toward fulfillment and growth.[33]

FEAR MODULATION: TAMING THE BEAST WITHIN

Fear, with its primal grip, can paralyze us, imprisoning us in a cage of apprehension and doubt. Yet, within the recesses of the prefrontal cortex lies the key to liberation—the power to modulate our response to fear with reason and rationality. By tempering the amygdala's primal response to perceived threats, the prefrontal cortex empowers us to confront adversity with courage and resilience, transforming fear into an opportunity for growth and self-discovery.

INTUITION: THE WISDOM OF THE HEART

In decision-making, intuition serves as our silent guide, whispering wisdom from the depths of our being. Guided by the subtle whispers of the heart, facilitated by the prefrontal cortex, we navigate the labyrinth of choice confidently and clearly. In the sanctuary of intuition, logic yields to intuition, and certainty gives way to trust, illuminating the path toward our true purpose and destiny.[34]

MORALITY:
NAVIGATING THE ETHICAL LANDSCAPE

In a world fraught with moral ambiguity, the prefrontal cortex serves as our moral compass, guiding us toward ethical clarity and integrity. Through its discerning gaze, we grasp the broader ethical context of our actions, aligning our behavior with the dictates of conscience and the greater good. In the crucible of moral decision-making, we transcend the narrow confines of self-interest, embracing the timeless principles of justice, compassion, and virtue.[35]

The Theory of MAGNUS OVEA will account for the importance of building capacities among these nine (9) functions of the prefrontal cortex. The theory will claim that to elevate our GREAT to MAGNUS, one needs to *Over-Excel Attunement* (OVEA).

CHAPTER 7

NEUROBIOLOGICAL FOUNDATIONS OF BEHAVIORAL DYNAMICS: INTEGRATING SIEGEL'S ATTUNEMENT WITH BANDURA'S AND VROOM'S THEORIES

Dr. Daniel Siegel's groundbreaking work on the Science of Attunement offers a profound neurobiological perspective that enriches our comprehension of the intricate interplay between cognition, emotion, and behavior, as expounded in the seminal theories of Albert Bandura's Social Cognitive Theory and Social Learning Theory and Victor Vroom's Expectancy Theory.

- **Attuned Communication and Empathy:** Siegel underscores the significance of attuned communication in nurturing genuine connections and empathy among individuals. This notion closely resonates with Bandura's concept of observational learning, where individuals acquire new behaviors by observing others. Furthermore, Siegel's emphasis on empathy mirrors Bandura's notion of modeling, suggesting that individuals can understand and resonate with others' emotions through observing and imitating empathic behaviors.

- **Emotional Balance and Fear Modulation:** Siegel delves into the neurobiology of emotional regulation, particularly highlighting the role of the prefrontal cortex in maintaining emotional equilibrium and modulating fear responses. This insight parallels Bandura's emphasis on self-regulation within Social Cognitive Theory, wherein individuals actively monitor and adjust their thoughts, emotions, and behaviors to attain desired outcomes. Similarly, Vroom's Expectancy Theory acknowledges the influence of individuals' beliefs regarding the consequences of their actions, which can significantly impact their emotional responses and fear modulation.

- **Response Flexibility and Intuition:** Siegel elucidates the remarkable capacity of the prefrontal cortex for response flexibility and intuitive decision-making, enabling individuals to pause, reflect, and consciously choose their actions. This aligns with Bandura's emphasis on self-regulation and cognitive processes within Social Cognitive Theory, wherein individuals engage in deliberate action based on their observations and cognitive appraisals. Additionally, Vroom's theory underscores the role of individuals' expectations and motivations in shaping intuitive decision-making processes within organizational contexts.

- **Insight and Morality:** Siegel's exploration of insight and morality is a vital bridge to Bandura's emphasis on self-efficacy and moral decision-making within Social Cognitive Theory. Individuals' insights into their cognitive processes and ethical considerations align closely with Bandura's concept of self-regulation and reciprocal determinism, wherein personal factors and environmental impacts influence moral behavior. Furthermore, Vroom's Expectancy Theory acknowledges the effects of individuals' valence, or the perceived value of ethical considerations, on their motivation to act ethically within organizational settings.

In essence, Siegel's Science of Attunement offers a robust neurobiological foundation for comprehending the cognitive, emotional, and behavioral processes elucidated in Bandura's Social Cognitive Theory, Social Learning Theory, and Vroom's Expectancy Theory.

By integrating these perspectives, we comprehensively understand human behavior and motivation, informed by psychological and neurobiological insights. This synthesis enriches our theoretical knowledge and presents profound implications for practical applications in fields ranging from education to organizational management.

CHAPTER 8
MAGNUS OVEA THEORY

As mentioned briefly in the introduction chapter of this book, **MAGNUS OVEA Theory** is a groundbreaking paradigm poised to revolutionize our understanding of human performance and well-being.

The theory transcends traditional boundaries, offering actionable, teachable, and quantifiable insights into the expansive realm of human potential. At its core, the MAGNUS OVEA Theory is a theory of theories.

This meta-framework operationalizes and synthesizes Bandura and Vroom's foundational works, rendering them accessible and applicable across diverse domains of human endeavor. It leverages the power of attunement—a concept central to Siegel's neurobiological framework—to enable full functionality of human agency, generating energy and outcomes of unparalleled significance.

Through meticulous examination and synthesis, the MAGNUS OVEA Theory unveils a comprehensive framework meticulously designed to navigate the intricate tapestry of individual and collective agency. Spanning the 11 Rings of Performance (outlined in length in the next chapter), each domain represents a facet of mastery—each a ring in the ladder to excellence:

- **Ring 1—Relationship Development (RD)—** Nurturing meaningful connections and fostering interpersonal harmony.
- **Ring 2—Family Dynamics (FD)—**Cultivating resilience and cohesion within familial relationships.
- **Ring 3—Spiritual Being (SB)—**Exploring and nurturing the spiritual dimensions of existence.
- **Ring 4—Mental Toughness (MT)—**Cultivating cognitive fortitude and adaptability.
- **Ring 5—Emotional Factor (EF)—**Enhancing emotional intelligence and regulation.
- **Ring 6—Physical Health Optimization (PHO)—** Prioritizing physical well-being and vitality.
- **Ring 7—Resilience Fitness (RF)—**Developing tenacity and flexibility in adversity.
- **Ring 8—Financial Stability (FS)—**Fostering financial literacy and security.
- **Ring 9—Occupational Fulfillment (OF)—**Finding purpose and satisfaction in one's career or vocation.
- **Ring 10—Leadership Capabilities (LC)—**Cultivating practical leadership skills and influence.
- **Ring 11—Social Connections (SC)—**Building networks and fostering community engagement.

Dynamic terrain within each ring is central to the MAGNUS OVEA Theory. Fluid landscapes encompass the diverse social, psychological, and situational factors shaping human behavior and outcomes. Acknowledging the complexity and fluidity of human experience, this theory empowers individuals to adapt and navigate with agility, optimizing their chances of success in any endeavor.

Within this theoretical framework lies a transformative proposition: true evolution begins with a candid confrontation of one's internal landscape. It challenges individuals to journey from mediocrity to greatness, compelling them to transcend their limitations and ascend to excellence. The MAGNUS OVEA Theory asserts that individuals unlock their latent potential by recognizing and elevating their internal landscape, propelling them toward unprecedented achievement and fulfillment.

As individuals traverse the crucible of self-improvement, they encounter many challenges within each ring, each presenting its unique trials and tribulations. Yet, within this crucible of perseverance, the MAGNUS emerges—a symbol of unparalleled excellence, a testament to the boundless potential of the human spirit. Each page of this discourse invites readers on a voyage of discovery, challenging preconceptions, expanding horizons, and igniting dormant potential.

CHAPTER 9

THE JUSTIFICATION OF THE MAGNUS OVEA THEORY

The interconnectedness and interoperability of these 11 RINGS of MAGNUS OVEA form a comprehensive framework rooted in Bandura's Social Learning and Cognitive Theories while embodying Daniel Siegel's science of attunement, making it evidence-based and interdisciplinary. Its operationalization optimizes human potential, fosters resilience, and cultivates enduring well-being across all dimensions of life.

- **Theoretical Underpinnings**: The theory is grounded in well-established concepts and principles from diverse fields such as psychology, sociology, health sciences, and organizational behavior. It draws upon existing theoretical frameworks related to human performance, wellness, and resilience, integrating these concepts into a unified model.

- **Evidence-Based Support**: Each component of the MAGNUS OVEA theory is supported by empirical research and evidence-based practices from a wide array of scientific disciplines. The references provided in the theory highlight the extensive body of literature and research studies that substantiate the interconnectedness of the theory's components and their impact on human performance.

- **Interconnected Nature**: The theory elucidates the interconnectedness of 11 distinct RINGS of human performance and well-being, demonstrating how each dimension influences and interacts. This integrated approach aligns with the criteria of an encompassing theory that accounts for the multifaceted nature of human existence and functioning.

- **Practical Implications**: The theory has practical implications for interventions, programs, and strategies to enhance human performance and well-being. Its evidence-based foundation and integrated nature make it applicable in diverse contexts, such as clinical settings, workplace environments, educational institutions, and community development initiatives.

- **Holistic Perspective**: The MAGNUS OVEA Theory encompasses multiple domains of human experience, from social relationships to spiritual well-being, physical health, and occupational fulfillment. This holistic perspective provides a comprehensive view of human performance and well-being, addressing various aspects of individual and collective functioning.

- **Predictive and Explanatory Power**: The theory's interconnected rings provide a framework for understanding and predicting behaviors, peak performance, and well-being.

By emphasizing the relationships and interactions between its components, the theory offers explanatory depth in elucidating the complexities of the human experience.

PART II
11 RINGS OF MAGNUS OVEA

"Peak performance is a symphony of excellence, a crescendo of mastery that harmonizes with the gentle rhythm of well-being. It is not merely the attainment of becoming more but the artful dance between achievement and self-care, where each step forward is met with a mindful pause for rejuvenation. In this delicate balance, success is not measured solely by the heights we reach but by the depth of our vitality and resilience. True mastery is not found in relentless pursuit alone, but in the tender nurturing of our physical, mental, and emotional landscapes, ensuring that each summit is met with a renewed sense of purpose and joy."

CHAPTER 10

RING 1

Relationship Development (RD): Nurturing Meaningful Connections and Fostering Interpersonal Harmony

Relationship Development (RD) is the 1st RING of MAGNUS OVEA, a pivotal force propelling us forward. The Dynamic Terrains (DT) of mastering the art of relationship development illuminate the RING's profound significance in fostering individual well-being and catalyzing peak performance. It unveils the compelling truth at the heart of every successful career and enriching existence: the strength of our connections directly shapes the trajectory of our happiness and achievements. From the intricate web of friendships to the complicated networks of professional alliances, the tapestry of our lives is woven with threads of interpersonal bonds. Thus, it becomes abundantly clear that nurturing and cultivating these relationships is not merely a choice but a fundamental necessity for navigating the complexities of contemporary life with resilience and grace.[36]

 RDDT 1—Self-Reflection (Relationship Development Dynamic Terrains # 1) is a profoundly reflective process that is the cornerstone for cultivating self-awareness and fostering meaningful connections with others. It involves taking a conscious and deliberate pause to examine our thoughts, emotions, beliefs, behaviors, and underlying motivations and implications. Through self-reflection, we gain valuable insights into our values, strengths, and areas for growth, allowing us to navigate life's complexities with greater clarity and purpose. Moreover, self-reflection enables us to develop empathy and understanding towards others by recognizing commonalities in our human experiences and appreciating diverse perspectives. By engaging in regular self-reflection, we create space for personal growth, transformation, and the cultivation of deeper connections with ourselves and those around us.[37]

 RDDT 2—Active Listening (Relationship Development Dynamic Terrains # 2) transcends being merely a communication technique; it serves as a vital bridge to fostering profound understanding, authentic connection, and enduring trust between individuals. It entails more than just passively hearing words; it involves wholeheartedly engaging with the speaker, immersing oneself in their words, and comprehending their message on a deeper level. Active listening requires attentive concentration and empathetic understanding as listeners strive to grasp the speaker's emotions, intentions, and underlying perspectives. Moreover, active listening entails thoughtful responses validating the

speaker's experiences and feelings while nurturing empathy and mutual respect. Crucially, active listening involves vigorously committing to remembering and internalizing the content of the conversation, conveying a genuine investment in the relationship, and fostering a sense of connection and trust. In essence, active listening transcends verbal exchange; it cultivates an environment of openness, empathy, and reciprocity, laying the groundwork for meaningful relationships and authentic communication.[38]

 RDDT 3—Effective Communication (Relationship Development Dynamic Terrains # 3) is the essential thread weaving through the intricate tapestry of successful relationships, seamlessly connecting individuals, and aligning teams with clarity, cohesion, and purpose. It transcends mere exchanges of words, encompassing active listening, empathetic understanding, and clear expression of thoughts and feelings. Effective communication allows individuals to share ideas, collaborate on projects, and resolve conflicts quickly and efficiently. Moreover, it fosters trust, respect, and mutual understanding, nurturing strong bonds and fostering a sense of belonging within teams and communities. Effective communication intricately stitches together diverse perspectives and experiences like a skilled weaver, creating a cohesive tapestry of shared goals, values, and aspirations. Ultimately, it empowers individuals and teams to navigate challenges, seize opportunities, and achieve collective success, serving as the cornerstone of harmonious and fulfilling relationships.[39]

 RDDT 4—Conflict Resolution (Relationship Development Dynamic Terrains # 4) stands as the indispensable process of seeking peaceful resolutions to disagreements, serving as a crucial skill for nurturing healthy, productive relationships across personal and professional

realms. It encompasses addressing conflicts and descents with sensitivity, empathy, and open-mindedness, aiming to resolve immediate disputes and strengthen rapport and understanding between parties. Conflict resolution promotes mutual respect, trust, and cooperation by fostering constructive dialogue, active listening, and collaborative problem-solving. Moreover, it empowers individuals and teams to navigate differences effectively, promoting resilience and adaptability amidst diverse perspectives and interests. As a cornerstone of interpersonal dynamics, conflict resolution paves the way for harmonious interactions, sustainable agreements, and shared success, ensuring the vitality and vitality of relationships in all spheres of life.[40]

 RDDT 5—Trust and Rapport (Relationship Development Dynamic Terrains # 5) are closely intertwined concepts that often complement each other in interpersonal relationships. Trust refers to a firm belief in the reliability, truth, or ability of someone or something. It involves confidence and faith in another person's integrity, honesty, and intentions. Trust is built over time through consistent actions, reliability, and transparency in communication and behavior. Conversely, rapport refers to a harmonious and sympathetic relationship characterized by mutual understanding, empathy, and respect. It involves a sense of connection and ease in communication between individuals, where they feel comfortable expressing themselves openly and honestly. Trust and rapport create a strong foundation for healthy and meaningful relationships. Trust establishes the reliability and credibility necessary for individuals to feel secure, while rapport fosters a sense of closeness and understanding that enhances communication and mutual respect. Building trust and rapport is essential for fostering genuine connections and cooperation in personal and professional interactions.[41]

RDDT 6—Feedback and Coaching (Relationship Development Dynamic Terrains # 6) are integral components of personal and professional development, often working hand in hand to support growth and improvement. Feedback involves providing specific information to an individual about their performance, behavior, or outcomes. It can be positive, reinforcing desired behaviors or outcomes, and constructive, highlighting areas for improvement. Effective feedback is timely, specific, and actionable, focusing on behaviors rather than personal attributes. It aims to facilitate learning and development by offering insights into strengths and areas needing improvement. Conversely, coaching is a supportive and collaborative process aimed at helping individuals reach their full potential. It involves guiding, challenging, and empowering individuals to set and achieve goals, overcome obstacles, and develop new skills. Coaches provide guidance, encouragement, and accountability, fostering self-awareness and self-directed learning. Coaching can take various forms, such as one-on-one sessions, group workshops, or mentorship relationships. Feedback and coaching create a dynamic framework for continuous learning and improvement. Feedback provides valuable insights and guidance, while coaching offers personalized support and encouragement in applying feedback to achieve goals and enhance performance. By integrating feedback and coaching into personal and professional development efforts, individuals can cultivate their strengths, address areas for growth, and achieve tremendous success.[42]

 RDDT 7—Collaboration (Relationship Development Dynamic Terrains # 7) is the cornerstone of effective teamwork and organizational success. When individuals come together and synergize their talents, skills, and perspectives, they can achieve outcomes that surpass what each person could accomplish individually. Collaboration fosters innovation,

creativity, and problem-solving by leveraging team members' collective intelligence and diverse experiences. By embracing collaboration, teams can tap into a wealth of ideas, knowledge, and resources, leading to more comprehensive solutions and better decision-making. Moreover, collaboration promotes a sense of belonging, trust, and mutual respect among team members, enhancing communication and cooperation. In today's interconnected and fast-paced world, collaboration is essential for organizations to adapt to change, stay competitive, and thrive. It enables teams to navigate complex challenges, seize opportunities, and achieve shared goals effectively. Ultimately, collaboration is not just about working together; it's about attaining synergy and unlocking the full potential of individuals and teams to create something truly remarkable.[43]

 RDDT 8—Cultural Competencies and Diversity (Relationship Development Dynamic Terrains # 8) refers to a state of unity or collective action involving multiple individuals, groups, or entities. It implies collaboration, cooperation, and mutual support towards a common goal or purpose. In cultural competencies and diversity, "together" emphasizes the importance of inclusivity, collaboration, and respect for differences within a diverse community or organization. Cultural competencies refer to the knowledge, skills, and attitudes required to effectively interact and work with people from diverse cultural backgrounds. It involves understanding, valuing, and respecting cultural differences and being able to adapt and communicate sensitively across cultures. Diversity encompasses the variety of differences among individuals, including but not limited to race, ethnicity, gender, sexual orientation, religion, age, socioeconomic status, and abilities. Embracing diversity

means recognizing and appreciating each individual's unique perspectives, experiences, and contributions. Together, cultural competencies and diversity emphasize the importance of fostering an inclusive environment where people from diverse backgrounds feel valued, respected, and empowered to contribute their perspectives and talents. It involves building bridges across cultural divides, promoting equity and justice, and leveraging the richness of diversity to drive innovation and growth.[44]

 RDDT 9—A Growth Mindset (Relationship Development Dynamic Terrains # 9) believes that abilities, intelligence, and talents are not fixed traits but can be developed through dedication, effort, and learning. Individuals with a growth mindset approach challenges as opportunities for growth, demonstrating resilience, persistence, and a willingness to learn from setbacks and criticism. They understand that innate abilities do not solely determine success but are shaped by effort and perseverance. Inspired by the success of others, they embrace learning, continuously seeking new challenges and opportunities for self-improvement. A growth mindset fosters a belief in one's potential for growth and development, leading to increased motivation and tremendous success in various areas of life.[45]

 RDDT 10—Leadership and Vision (Relationship Development Dynamic Terrains # 10) are intertwined concepts essential for guiding individuals and organizations toward a shared purpose and desired future. Leadership involves inspiring, influencing, and motivating others to achieve common goals. At the same time, vision encompasses the ability to envision a compelling future state and articulate a clear path. Effective leadership involves providing direction and guidance and fostering trust, collaboration, and empowerment within a team or organization.

Leaders with vision can see beyond the present circumstances and imagine possibilities for growth, innovation, and positive change. They communicate their vision in a way that inspires and engages others, rallying support and commitment toward its realization. Leadership and vision complement each other in driving organizational and personal success. Leaders with a clear vision provide a sense of purpose and direction, aligning the efforts of individuals toward common objectives. They inspire confidence and enthusiasm, motivating others to overcome challenges and pursue ambitious goals. Additionally, leaders who embody their vision through their actions and decisions inspire trust and credibility, reinforcing their influence and impact.[46]

RELATIONSHIP DEVELOPMENT HABIT-BUILDING ACTIONABLE TAKEAWAYS

1. **Self-Reflection:** Dedicate time to introspection to clarify your values, strengths, and areas for growth, fostering deeper connections with yourself and others.

2. **Active Listening:** Engage wholeheartedly with others, immersing yourself in their words to foster understanding, empathy, and trust in your relationships.

3. **Effective Communication:** Master the art of clear and empathetic communication, building trust and alignment within teams and communities.

4. **Conflict Resolution:** Approach conflicts with openness and empathy, aiming for peaceful resolutions that strengthen rapport and understanding.

5. **Trust and Rapport:** Cultivate trust through consistent actions and transparency, fostering harmonious relationships grounded in mutual respect and understanding.

6. **Feedback and Coaching:** Embrace feedback and coaching as catalysts for personal and professional growth, leveraging insights and support to reach your full potential.

7. **Collaboration:** Harness the collective intelligence and diverse perspectives of teams to achieve innovative solutions and shared success.

8. **Cultural Competencies and Diversity:** Foster inclusivity and respect for diversity, creating environments where every voice is valued and heard.

9. **Growth Mindset:** Adopt a continuous learning and growth mindset, embracing challenges as opportunities for development and success.

10. **Leadership and Vision:** Inspire and empower others toward a shared vision, leading with purpose and clarity to drive meaningful change.

11. **Empathy and Understanding:** Cultivate empathy and understanding toward others' perspectives and experiences, fostering deeper connections and mutual respect.

12. **Flexibility and Adaptability:** Be open to change and willing to adapt your communication and approach to meet the needs of diverse individuals and situations.

13. **Patience and Compassion:** Practice patience and compassion in your interactions, recognizing that everyone has unique journeys and challenges.

14. **Boundaries and Respect:** Establish clear boundaries and respect others' boundaries, fostering healthy and respectful relationships built on trust and autonomy.

15. **Gratitude and Appreciation:** Express gratitude and appreciation for the relationships in your life, nurturing a culture of kindness and gratitude.

By integrating these takeaways into your relational practices and mindset, you can cultivate deeper connections, foster meaningful collaborations, and navigate the complexities of life with resilience and grace. Remember, relationships are the cornerstone of a fulfilling life, and investing in their development is a journey well worth undertaking.

RING 1: Relationship Development

01	Self-Reflection	
02	Active Listening	
03	Effective Communications	
04	Conflict Resolution	
05	Trust and Rapport	
06	Feedback and Coaching	
07	Collaboration	
08	Cultural Competencies and Diversity	
09	Growth Mindset	
10	Leadership and Vision	

CHAPTER 11

RING 2

Family Dynamics (FD): Cultivating Resilience and Cohesion Within Familial Relationships

Family Dynamics (FD), the 2nd RING of MAGNUS OVEA, is the cornerstone of our social and emotional framework, intricately shaping our identities and experiences. The profound Dynamic Terrains (DT) of the RING improve our understanding and navigate family dynamics, revealing its indispensable role in fostering individual growth and collective well-being. From the bonds forged in childhood to the complexities of adult relationships, the dynamics within our families profoundly influence our perceptions, behaviors, and aspirations. At its essence, this exploration underscores the vital truth that the quality of our familial connections profoundly impacts our overall happiness and fulfillment. By unraveling the complexities of family dynamics, we gain insight into the intricate interplay of love, conflict, support, and resilience that characterize the family unit. Thus, recognizing and nurturing healthy family dynamics is a cornerstone of personal development and a critical determinant of societal harmony and progress.[47]

 FDDT 1—Openness (Family Dynamics Dynamic Terrains # 1) within the family dynamic refers to an environment of transparency, honesty, and communication. It involves family members feeling comfortable expressing their thoughts, feelings, and concerns openly and without fear of judgment. In an open family dynamic, there is a willingness to listen, understand, and respect each other's perspectives, even during disagreements or conflicts. Openness fosters trust, intimacy, and mutual support among family members, creating a sense of belonging and emotional connection. It also encourages collaboration and problem-solving, as family members work together to address challenges and navigate life's ups and downs. Overall, openness within the family dynamic strengthens relationships, promotes resilience, and nurtures a supportive and nurturing family environment.[48]

 FDDT 2—Listening and Understanding (Family Dynamics Dynamic Terrains # 2) within a family are fundamental aspects of healthy communication and relationships. Listening involves hearing the words spoken by family members and actively paying attention to their thoughts, feelings, and needs. It requires empathy, patience, and a genuine interest in understanding the perspective of others. Understanding goes beyond simply hearing what is said; it involves interpreting and empathizing with the emotions, intentions, and underlying meaning behind the

words. In a family setting, listening and understanding create a supportive and nurturing environment where each member feels valued, respected, and heard. When family members listen attentively to each other, they demonstrate care and consideration, building trust and strengthening bonds. Understanding fosters empathy and compassion, allowing family members to connect on a deeper level and validate each other's experiences and feelings. Listening and understanding within a family helps resolve conflicts, prevent misunderstandings, and foster harmony and cooperation. It promotes open communication, problem-solving, and the building of strong, resilient relationships that withstand the test of time. Ultimately, listening and understanding within a family lay the foundation for love, trust, and mutual support, enriching the family dynamic and enhancing overall well-being.[49]

 FDDT 3—Conflict Resolution (Family Dynamics Dynamic Terrains # 3) within a family involves addressing disagreements and tensions constructively, aiming to reach a mutually beneficial solution while preserving relationships. It requires open and honest communication, active listening, empathy, and a willingness to understand each other's perspectives. By identifying the root causes of conflicts, brainstorming solutions, and engaging in negotiation and compromise, family members can work together to find resolutions that meet the needs and interests of everyone involved. Effective conflict resolution fosters trust, respect, and harmony within the family, promoting more robust relationships and overall well-being.[50]

 FDDT 4—Support and Encouragement (Family Dynamics Dynamic Terrains # 4) within a family are essential to nurturing relationships and fostering emotional well-being. Support involves helping, comforting, and understanding family members during challenging

times, whether through practical help, emotional reassurance, or simply being there to listen. Encouragement entails providing positive reinforcement, praise, and motivation to help family members pursue their goals, overcome obstacles, and realize their potential. In a supportive and encouraging family environment, individuals feel valued, accepted, and empowered to be themselves and pursue their aspirations. Family members unite and uplift each other, celebrate successes, and provide strength and resilience during challenging moments. This support and encouragement contribute to a sense of belonging, connection, and love within the family, laying the foundation for personal growth, happiness, and fulfillment.[51]

 FDDT 5—Quality Time and Engagement (Family Dynamics Dynamic Terrains # 5) within a family are vital for nurturing strong bonds, fostering communication, and creating cherished memories. Quality time involves dedicating focused attention and presence to shared activities, conversations, and experiences, free from distractions. It's about making meaningful connections and building relationships through genuine interaction and mutual enjoyment. Engagement within a family extends beyond mere presence to active participation and involvement in each other's lives. It includes listening attentively, offering support and encouragement, and participating in activities that reflect shared interests and values. Whether engaging in fun outings, mealtime conversations, or meaningful traditions, quality time and engagement strengthen familial ties, promote understanding, and create a sense of belonging and unity within the family unit. By prioritizing these moments, families can cultivate a deep sense of connection, resilience, and love that enriches their lives.[52]

FDDT 6—Respect and Boundaries (Family Dynamics Dynamic Terrains # 6) within a family are essential for maintaining healthy relationships, fostering autonomy, and ensuring mutual understanding and harmony. Respect involves recognizing and valuing each family member's individuality, opinions, and feelings, even in times of disagreement. It means treating each other with dignity, empathy, and consideration while refraining from judgment or criticism. Boundaries establish clear guidelines and expectations for personal space, privacy, and autonomy within the family unit. They define acceptable behavior and communication, helping to prevent conflicts and misunderstandings. Respecting boundaries means honoring each family member's need for autonomy, consent, and self-expression while recognizing and communicating one's boundaries. By fostering respect and honoring boundaries, families create a safe and supportive environment where individuals feel valued, understood, and empowered to thrive.[53]

FDDT 7—Flexibility and Adaptability (Family Dynamics Dynamic Terrains # 7) are indispensable qualities in navigating the complexities of family life, especially in the face of change, challenges, and varying circumstances. Flexibility involves being open-minded and willing to adjust plans, routines, and expectations to accommodate evolving needs and priorities within the family. It requires a willingness to compromise, problem-solve, and explore new solutions when faced with unexpected situations or transitions. Adaptability encompasses the ability to respond effectively to changes in roles, dynamics, and circumstances, embracing them as opportunities for growth and learning. It involves resilience, creativity, and a positive attitude towards managing uncertainties and transitions. Flexibility and adaptability enable individuals to navigate diverse needs, preferences, and personalities in family life, fostering resilience, harmony, and mutual support. By cultivating these qualities,

families can thrive amidst life's inevitable ups and downs, building stronger bonds and creating lasting memories.[54]

 FDDT 8—Trust and Reliability (Family Dynamics Dynamic Terrains # 8) are foundational pillars of solid family relationships, fostering a sense of security, intimacy, and mutual support. Trust within a family involves having confidence in each other's integrity, honesty, and intentions, knowing that family members can be relied upon to honor commitments, keep promises, and act with goodwill towards one another. On the other hand, reliability entails consistently demonstrating dependability, consistency, and accountability in actions and behaviors. It involves being there for each other, supporting, and following through on obligations and responsibilities. In a family built on trust and reliability, individuals feel safe to be themselves, express their thoughts and feelings openly, and rely on one another during joyful moments and times of adversity. These qualities strengthen bonds, cultivate resilience, and create a nurturing environment where love, respect, and understanding thrive.[55]

 FDDT 9—Empathy and Compassion (Family Dynamics Dynamic Terrains # 9) within a family are fundamental for fostering understanding, connection, and emotional support among its members. Empathy involves the ability to understand and share the feelings and perspectives of others, allowing family members to resonate with each other's experiences and emotions. It entails active listening, perspective-taking, and validating the feelings of loved ones, even when they differ from one's own. Compassion, on the other hand, is the genuine concern for the well-being and suffering of others, motivating acts of kindness, support, and care. Within a family, empathy and compassion create a supportive and nurturing atmosphere where individuals feel seen,

heard, and understood. They promote forgiveness, acceptance, and resilience, strengthening bonds and fostering a sense of belonging and unity. By embodying empathy and compassion, family members cultivate deeper connections, build trust, and navigate challenges with love and understanding.[56]

 FDDT 10—Shared Values and Goals (Family Dynamics Dynamic Terrains # 10) within a family provide a sense of purpose, unity, and direction, guiding collective actions and decisions towards common aspirations and principles. Shared values represent the beliefs, principles, and ethical standards that family members collectively uphold and prioritize. These may include values such as honesty, respect, integrity, compassion, or perseverance, which are the foundation for familial relationships and interactions. Shared goals, on the other hand, represent the desired outcomes or achievements that family members collaboratively strive towards. These goals could encompass various aspects of life, such as education, career, health, relationships, or personal development, reflecting the family's collective aspirations and priorities. Families create a cohesive framework for decision-making, problem-solving, and growth by aligning values and goals. They foster a sense of belonging, mutual support, and accountability, inspiring collaboration and resilience to pursue shared dreams and aspirations. Ultimately, shared values and goals strengthen familial bonds, nurture a sense of identity and belonging, and provide a roadmap for shared success and fulfillment.[57]

FAMILY DYNAMICS HABIT-BUILDING ACTIONABLE TAKEAWAYS

1. **Openness:** Foster an environment of transparency and communication within your family, where each member feels comfortable expressing thoughts and feelings without fear of judgment.
2. **Listening and Understanding:** Cultivate active listening skills and empathy to foster deeper connections and mutual understanding among family members.
3. **Conflict Resolution:** Approach conflicts constructively, aiming to find mutually beneficial solutions while preserving relationships.
4. **Support and Encouragement:** Help, comfort, and motivate family members, fostering resilience and personal growth.
5. **Quality Time and Engagement:** Dedicate focused attention to shared activities and conversations, strengthening familial bonds and creating cherished memories.
6. **Respect and Boundaries:** Recognize and honor each family member's individuality and boundaries, fostering mutual respect and understanding.
7. **Flexibility and Adaptability:** Embrace change and uncertainty with an open mind, fostering resilience and harmony within the family unit.
8. **Trust and Reliability:** Build trust through consistent actions and reliability, creating a secure and supportive family environment.

9. **Empathy and Compassion:** Practice active empathy and compassion towards family members, fostering understanding and emotional support.

10. **Shared Values and Goals:** Align on common values and aspirations as a family, providing a sense of purpose and unity in collective endeavors.

11. **Patience and Forgiveness:** Exercise patience and forgiveness in conflict or misunderstanding, promoting healing and reconciliation.

12. **Communication Skills:** Develop practical communication skills to express thoughts, feelings, and needs openly and respectfully.

13. **Celebration and Acknowledgment:** Recognize and celebrate each other's achievements and milestones, reinforcing a culture of appreciation and support.

14. **Individuality and Autonomy:** Honor and respect each family member's unique identity and autonomy, allowing space for personal growth and self-expression.

15. **Continuous Growth and Learning:** Embrace opportunities for growth and learning as a family, adapting and evolving together through life's challenges and triumphs.

By embodying these takeaways and integrating them into your family dynamics, you can nurture strong bonds, promote resilience, and cultivate a supportive and harmonious family environment. Remember, family is not just a unit; it's a sanctuary of love, understanding, and growth, where each member plays a vital role in shaping a shared journey of happiness and fulfillment.

RING 2: Family Dynamics

01	Openness	
02	Listening and Understanding	
03	Conflict Resolution	
04	Support and Encouragement	
05	Quality Time and Engagement	
06	Respect and Boundaries	
07	Flexibility and Adaptability	
08	Trust and Reliability	
09	Empathy and Compassion	
10	Shared Values and Goals	

CHAPTER 12

RING 3

Spiritual Being (SB): Exploring and Nurturing the Spiritual Dimensions of Existence

Spiritual Being (SB) emerges as the 3rd RING of MAGNUS OVEA, a profound essence of our existence that guides our quest for meaning, purpose, and connection with the transcendent. The Dynamic Terrains (DT) of the RING help us understand and nurture our spiritual being, illuminating its profound significance in shaping our inner landscapes and guiding our outer journeys. Beyond the confines of organized religion, spirituality encompasses a profoundly personal exploration of the mysteries of existence and the pursuit of transcendence. It acknowledges the inherent interconnectedness of all life forms and invites us to cultivate a sense of reverence, awe, and gratitude for the wonders of the universe. This exploration reveals that nurturing our spiritual being is a journey of self-discovery and a transformative path toward wholeness and harmony with the cosmos. By embracing our spiritual essence, we embark on a journey of profound inner healing, growth, and awakening, ultimately enriching our lives and fostering greater compassion and empathy toward all beings.[58]

 SBDT 1—Mindfulness and Presence (Spiritual Being Dynamic Terrains # 1) within the framework of spiritual being entailed cultivating heightened awareness and conscious engagement with the present moment, free from judgment or attachment to past or future events. It involves acknowledging and fully experiencing one's thoughts, emotions, and sensations as they arise while maintaining a sense of inner tranquility and acceptance. This practice encourages a deep connection to the essence of one's being, fostering a greater understanding of the interconnectedness of all life and the divine presence within and around us. Through mindfulness and presence, individuals can tap into a profound spiritual fulfillment, finding solace, guidance, and wisdom in the eternal now.[59]

 SBDT 2—Personal Beliefs (Spiritual Being Dynamic Terrains # 2) encompass the deeply held convictions, values, and principles that shape an individual's worldview and guide their actions and decisions. In the context of spiritual being, personal beliefs often reflect one's understanding of existence, purpose, and the nature of reality. These beliefs can encompass various aspects, such as religious faith, philosophical perspectives, moral codes, and metaphysical interpretations. Cultivating mindfulness and presence within the framework of personal beliefs involves embracing these convictions with open-mindedness, exploring their origins and implications, and striving for alignment between belief systems and

lived experiences. It entails being consciously aware of how these beliefs influence perceptions, interactions, and interpretations of the world while remaining open to growth, transformation, and the evolution of one's spiritual journey.[60]

 SBDT 3—Compassion and Kindness (Spiritual Being Dynamic Terrains # 3) are fundamental qualities (within the realm of spiritual beings), embodying the essence of empathy, benevolence, and altruism towards oneself and others. In this context, compassion involves recognizing and resonating with the suffering and struggles of fellow human beings, coupled with a genuine desire to alleviate that suffering and promote well-being. On the other hand, kindness encompasses acts of generosity, goodwill, and consideration towards all beings, rooted in a deep sense of interconnectedness and universal love. Cultivating mindfulness and presence with compassion and kindness involves cultivating a heart-centered awareness that embraces all life forms' inherent dignity and worth, fostering harmony, healing, and unity in the world. It entails embodying these virtues in thought, speech, and action and nurturing a compassionate presence that radiates peace, understanding, and acceptance wherever one goes.[61]

 SBDT 4—Inner Peace and Contentment (Spiritual Being Dynamic Terrains # 4) are the profound tranquility and fulfillment that arises from a deep sense of harmony, acceptance, and alignment with oneself and the world. In the context of spiritual being, inner peace refers to a serene state of mind that transcends external circumstances and is rooted in a profound awareness of one's true nature and purpose. Conversely, contentment involves finding satisfaction and joy in the present moment, free from the constant desires and attachments that often lead to suffering. Cultivating mindfulness and presence in conjunction with inner peace

and contentment entails cultivating a profound sense of self-awareness and acceptance, releasing resistance to the flow of life, and embracing each moment with gratitude and serenity. It involves recognizing that true peace and contentment come from within and are not dependent on external conditions, possessions, or achievements. Through meditation, self-reflection, and compassionate living, individuals can cultivate a lasting sense of inner peace and contentment that is a foundation for a meaningful and fulfilling life journey.[62]

 SBDT 5—Gratitude and Appreciation (Spiritual Being Dynamic Terrains # 5) are transformative attitudes that enrich the spiritual being, fostering a profound sense of connection, abundance, and joy. Gratitude involves acknowledging and recognizing the blessings, gifts, and opportunities in one's life, regardless of size or significance, and cultivating a heartfelt sense of thankfulness for them. On the other hand, appreciation involves recognizing the inherent value and beauty in the world around us, from the most superficial aspects of nature to the complexities of human relationships and experiences. Cultivating mindfulness and presence in conjunction with gratitude and appreciation entails cultivating a conscious awareness of the blessings and wonders of life, fostering an attitude of humility, wonder, and reverence towards the interconnected web of existence. It involves savoring each moment with awe and wonder and expressing gratitude and appreciation through acts of kindness, generosity, and service to others. By nurturing a grateful and appreciative heart, individuals can cultivate a more profound sense of fulfillment, connection, and purpose in their spiritual journey.[63]

 SBDT 6—Self-Awareness and Self-Reflection (Spiritual Being Dynamic Terrains # 6) are essential for deepening spiritual being and fostering insight, growth, and transformation. Self-awareness involves observing and

understanding one's thoughts, emotions, beliefs, and behaviors without judgment, allowing for a deeper understanding of oneself and one's inner dynamics. Self-reflection, on the other hand, involves actively engaging in introspection and contemplation to gain insight into one's experiences, motivations, and patterns of thought and behavior. Cultivating mindfulness and presence with self-awareness and self-reflection entails cultivating a spacious and non-reactive awareness that allows observing and exploring the inner landscape with curiosity and compassion. It involves creating regular stillness and solitude for introspection, journaling, meditation, or contemplative practices that foster self-inquiry and self-discovery. By developing a deeper understanding of oneself and one's inner world, individuals can cultivate greater clarity, authenticity, and alignment with their true essence, guiding them toward self-realization and spiritual fulfillment.[64]

 SBDT 7—Forgiveness and Letting Go (Spiritual Being Dynamic Terrains # 7) are transformative practices within spiritual beings, offering liberation from the burdens of resentment, anger, and pain and fostering inner peace and healing. Forgiveness involves releasing the desire for revenge or retribution and extending compassion and understanding towards oneself or others who have caused harm or suffering. On the other hand, letting go entails relinquishing attachment to past grievances, regrets, or expectations and embracing acceptance of what is, allowing for a sense of surrender and freedom from emotional entanglements. Cultivating mindfulness and presence in conjunction with forgiveness and letting go involves cultivating a compassionate and non-judgmental awareness of one's wounds and those of others, allowing space for forgiveness to arise naturally through self-reflection and empathy. It consists in recognizing that holding onto grudges or past hurts only perpetuates suffering and blocks the flow of love and healing in one's life. By practicing forgiveness and letting go, individuals can experience

profound liberation and transformation, opening their hearts to greater love, compassion, and inner peace and paving the way for more profound spiritual growth and connection.[65]

 SBDT 8—Service and Altruism (Spiritual Being Dynamic Terrains # 8) are integral aspects of a spiritual being, embodying the essence of compassion, generosity, and interconnectedness with all beings. Service involves selflessly contributing to the well-being and upliftment of others, whether through acts of kindness, volunteer work, or supporting charitable causes, motivated by a genuine desire to alleviate suffering and promote the greater good. Altruism, on the other hand, entails prioritizing the welfare of others above one's interests or passions, recognizing the inherent value and dignity of all beings and their interconnectedness in the web of existence. Cultivating mindfulness and presence in conjunction with service and altruism involves cultivating a heart-centered awareness that recognizes the needs and struggles of others and responds with empathy, kindness, and action. It consists of aligning one's actions and intentions with the principle of service to others, seeking opportunities to uplift and empower those in need, and contributing to creating a more compassionate and just world. By practicing service and altruism, individuals benefit others and experience a profound sense of fulfillment, purpose, and connection, deepening their spiritual journey and fostering a more harmonious and compassionate society.[66]

 SBDT 9—Connection with Nature and the Universe (Spiritual Being Dynamic Terrains # 9) is a profound aspect of spiritual being, encompassing a deep reverence, awe, and interconnectedness with the natural world and the cosmos. It involves recognizing that we are not separate from nature or the universe but rather an integral part of it, interconnected with all

living beings and the vastness of existence. Cultivating mindfulness and presence in conjunction with a connection to nature and the universe involves immersing oneself in the beauty and wonder of the natural world, whether through spending time in natural settings, practicing eco-friendly living, or contemplating the mysteries of the cosmos. It entails cultivating a sense of humility and gratitude for the abundance and diversity of life on Earth and the awe-inspiring grandeur of the universe. By nurturing a deep connection with nature and the universe, individuals can experience a profound sense of belonging, purpose, and interconnectedness, deepening their spiritual understanding and enriching their lives with meaning, wonder, and reverence for the sacredness of all creation.[67]

SBDT 10—Personal Growth (Spiritual Being Dynamic Terrains # 10) is an ongoing journey of self-discovery, learning, and development that contributes to expanding and evolving one's spiritual being. It involves cultivating self-awareness, challenging limiting beliefs, and embracing opportunities for growth and transformation. Personal growth encompasses various dimensions, including emotional, intellectual, relational, and spiritual growth, each contributing to a more holistic and fulfilling life experience. Cultivating mindfulness and presence with personal growth involves embracing a growth mindset, which sees challenges as opportunities for learning and development, and being open to feedback, self-reflection, and continuous improvement. It entails setting meaningful goals, stepping out of comfort zones, and engaging in practices that nurture self-compassion, resilience, and authenticity. By committing to a path of personal growth, individuals can unlock their full potential, cultivate greater self-fulfillment, and contribute positively to the world around them, ultimately enriching their spiritual journey and deepening their connection to the essence of their being.[68]

SPIRITUAL BEING HABIT-BUILDING ACTIONABLE TAKEAWAYS

1. **Mindfulness and Presence:** Cultivate a state of heightened awareness and conscious engagement with the present moment, fostering a deeper connection to the essence of your being.

2. **Personal Beliefs:** Embrace your convictions and values, exploring their origins and implications while remaining open to growth and evolution on your spiritual journey.

3. **Compassion and Kindness:** Practice empathy, benevolence, and altruism towards yourself and others, fostering harmony, healing, and unity in the world.

4. **Inner Peace and Contentment:** Find tranquility and fulfillment rooted in self-awareness, acceptance, and gratitude, recognizing that true peace comes from within.

5. **Gratitude and Appreciation:** Acknowledge the blessings and wonders of life, fostering humility, wonder, and reverence towards the interconnected web of existence.

6. **Self-Awareness and Self-Reflection:** Observe and understand your inner dynamics without judgment, fostering clarity, authenticity, and alignment with your true essence.

7. **Forgiveness and Letting Go:** Release the burdens of resentment and pain, embracing acceptance and freedom from emotional entanglements.

8. **Service and Altruism:** Contribute selflessly to the well-being of others, recognizing the interconnectedness of all beings and the greater good of humanity.

9. **Connection with Nature and the Universe:** Immerse yourself in the beauty and wonder of the natural world, cultivating reverence, awe, and interconnectedness with all creation.

10. **Personal Growth:** Commit to continuous learning and development, embracing challenges as opportunities for growth and transformation.

11. **Embrace Mystery and Wonder:** Embrace the mysteries of existence and the awe-inspiring grandeur of the cosmos, nurturing a sense of wonder and reverence for the sacredness of all creation.

12. **Practice Stillness and Solitude:** Create regular moments of stillness and solitude for contemplation, meditation, or introspection, allowing space for inner exploration and self-discovery.

13. **Live with Intention and Purpose:** Align your actions and intentions with your values and aspirations, living with purpose and meaning in each moment.

14. **Embody Authenticity and Integrity:** Live in alignment with your true essence, expressing yourself authentically and embodying integrity in all aspects of your life.

15. **Cultivate Love and Connection:** Foster deep connections with yourself, others, and the universe, nurturing a sense of love, belonging, and interconnectedness in your spiritual journey.

By embodying these takeaways and integrating them into your spiritual practice, you can deepen your connection to the essence of your being, foster greater harmony and fulfillment, and enrich your journey toward self-realization and spiritual awakening. Remember, spirituality is not a destination but a lifelong journey of discovery, growth, and transformation, inviting you to embrace the mysteries of existence and awaken to the profound interconnectedness of all life.

RING 3: Spiritual Being

01	Mindfulness and Presence	
02	Personal Beliefs	
03	Compassion and Kindness	
04	Inner Peace and Contentment	
05	Gratitude and Appreciation	
06	Self-awareness and Self-Reflection	
07	Forgiveness and Letting Go	
08	Service and Altruism	
09	Connection with Nature and Universe	
10	Personal Growth	

CHAPTER 13

RING 4

Mental Toughness (MT): Cultivating Cognitive Fortitude and Adaptability

Mental Toughness (MT), our 4th RING of MAGNUS OVEA, is the bedrock of resilience and peak performance, embodying the capacity to persevere and thrive in adversity. Below, we dive into the multifaceted Dynamic Terrains (DT) of mastering mental toughness, illuminating its profound significance in navigating life's challenges and achieving extraordinary feats. Beyond mere resilience, mental toughness encompasses a fusion of resilience, grit, and adaptability, empowering individuals to harness their inner strength and overcome obstacles with unwavering resolve. It acknowledges the inherent power of mindset and self-belief in shaping our responses to adversity, offering a roadmap for cultivating resilience and tenacity in pursuing our goals. At its essence, this exploration unveils mental toughness as a dynamic skill set that can be honed through deliberate practice and psychological training, enabling individuals to transcend their limitations and unleash their full potential. By embracing the principles of mental toughness, we unlock the keys to unlocking our inner greatness and navigating life's challenges with courage, confidence, and grace.[69]

 MTDT 1—Stress Tolerance and Resilience Growth (Mental Toughness Dynamic Terrains # 1) is the ability to withstand and adapt to adversities, challenges, and pressures without succumbing to negative consequences. Stress tolerance involves maintaining composure, clarity of thought, and effective decision-making under pressure. At the same time, resilience consists of returning from setbacks, failures, or stressful situations with renewed strength and determination. Mental toughness integrates these attributes, fostering a mindset that not only endures stress but thrives in the face of it, utilizing setbacks as opportunities for growth and development rather than obstacles. This amalgamation enables individuals to confront demanding circumstances with perseverance, adaptability, and an unwavering resolve to overcome obstacles and achieve goals.[70]

 MTDT 2—Emotional Regulation (Mental Toughness Dynamic Terrains # 2) is the capacity to manage and control one's emotions effectively, particularly in high-pressure or challenging situations. It involves recognizing, understanding, and appropriately channeling emotions to maintain focus, clarity, and optimal performance. Individuals adept in emotional regulation can navigate stress, setbacks, and intense situations without being overwhelmed by their emotions, thus preserving rationality and constructive thinking. This facet of mental toughness enables individuals

to stay composed, make sound decisions, and maintain resilience in the face of adversity, fostering a mindset conducive to achievement and success even amidst significant emotional strain.[71]

 MTDT 3—Persistence and Perseverance (Mental Toughness Dynamic Terrains # 3) are essential components of mental toughness, embodying the determination and resilience to pursue goals despite obstacles, setbacks, or failures. Persistence involves the sustained effort and tenacity to keep moving forward in the face of challenges, maintaining focus and commitment to achieving desired outcomes. Perseverance goes beyond mere persistence, encompassing the ability to endure hardships, setbacks, and repeated failures without losing sight of the ultimate objective. Mental toughness incorporates these qualities, empowering individuals to pursue their aspirations despite adversity, setbacks, or discouragement. It fosters a mindset that views challenges as opportunities for growth, learning, and eventual success. It drives individuals to push beyond their limits and achieve their goals through unwavering determination and resilience.[72]

 MTDT 4—Self-Confidence and Belief (Mental Toughness Dynamic Terrains # 4) are integral facets of mental toughness, embodying a strong sense of self-assurance and faith in one's abilities, even in the face of uncertainty or adversity. Self-confidence involves a deep trust in one's skills, knowledge, and capacity to succeed, empowering individuals to tackle challenges with assertiveness and conviction. Belief encompasses unwavering faith in one's vision, goals, and potential for achievement, fueling perseverance and resilience in pursuing objectives. Mental toughness integrates these attributes, fostering a mindset characterized by robust self-confidence and unshakable belief in one's capabilities and aspirations. This confidence and belief are foundational pillars,

providing individuals with the courage, motivation, and resilience to overcome obstacles, navigate adversity, and succeed in their endeavors.[73]

 MTDT 5—Focus and Concentration (Mental Toughness Dynamic Terrains # 5) are essential components of mental toughness, reflecting the ability to maintain attention and clarity of mind amidst distractions, challenges, and pressures. Focus involves directing one's attention and energy towards specific goals or tasks, minimizing distractions, and staying fully engaged in the present moment. Concentration goes hand in hand with focus, enabling individuals to channel their mental resources effectively, sustain attention over extended periods, and achieve optimal performance. Mental toughness integrates these attributes, fostering a mindset characterized by laser-like focus and unwavering concentration, even in adversity or uncertainty. This heightened focus and concentration empowers individuals to remain undeterred by distractions or setbacks, enabling them to pursue their objectives with precision, determination, and resilience, ultimately enhancing their ability to overcome obstacles and achieve success.[74]

 MTDT 6—Optimism and a Positive Attitude (Mental Toughness Dynamic Terrains # 6) are fundamental aspects of mental toughness, reflecting a proactive and hopeful perspective even amid challenges or setbacks. Optimism involves maintaining a positive outlook, believing in the potential for favorable outcomes, and viewing setbacks as temporary obstacles rather than insurmountable barriers. A positive attitude encompasses resilience, adaptability, and a constructive approach to adversity, fostering a mindset that seeks opportunities for growth and learning in every situation. Mental toughness integrates these qualities, nurturing an optimistic outlook and a positive attitude that enables individuals to maintain motivation, resilience, and perseverance in pursuing their

goals. This mindset enhances emotional well-being and empowers individuals to navigate difficulties with grace, confidence, and determination, ultimately facilitating tremendous success and fulfillment in their endeavors.[75]

MTDT 7—Problem-Solving and Creativity (Mental Toughness Dynamic Terrains # 7) are essential components of mental toughness, reflecting the ability to adaptively address challenges and generate innovative solutions in the face of adversity. Problem-solving involves identifying obstacles, analyzing situations, and devising effective strategies, often requiring critical thinking, logic, and resourcefulness. Creativity complements problem-solving by fostering the ability to think outside the box, explore unconventional approaches, and generate novel ideas or solutions. Mental toughness integrates these skills, cultivating a mindset that embraces challenges as opportunities for creative problem-solving and innovation. This mindset enables individuals to navigate obstacles with agility and resilience and empowers them to uncover new possibilities, capitalize on opportunities, and achieve success through inventive and resourceful approaches. By combining problem-solving with creativity, individuals can leverage their mental toughness to overcome adversity, adapt to change, and thrive in dynamic and challenging environments.[76]

MTDT 8—Goal Setting and Achievement (Mental Toughness Dynamic Terrains # 8) are central to mental toughness, embodying the ability to establish clear objectives, pursue them with determination, and ultimately succeed in their attainment. Goal setting involves defining specific, measurable, achievable, relevant, and time-bound (SMART) goals that align with one's values, aspirations, and capabilities. It requires careful planning, prioritization, and commitment to consistent

action toward desired outcomes. Achievement encompasses realizing these goals through persistent effort, resilience, and adaptability in facing obstacles or setbacks. Mental toughness integrates these processes, fostering a mindset characterized by goal clarity, resilience, and unwavering commitment to success. This mindset empowers individuals to set ambitious goals, navigate challenges with determination, and overcome barriers with creativity and perseverance, ultimately achieving their aspirations and fulfilling their potential. By harnessing their mental toughness, individuals can effectively translate their goals into tangible accomplishments, driving personal and professional growth and realizing lasting success.[77]

 MTDT 9—Adaptability and Flexibility (Mental Toughness Dynamic Terrains # 9) are crucial components of mental toughness, representing the capacity to adjust to changing circumstances, environments, or expectations with ease and resilience. Adaptability involves being open to new ideas, approaches, or challenges and pivoting when circumstances demand it. It requires assessing situations quickly, making informed decisions, and effectively modifying strategies or behaviors. Flexibility complements adaptability by enabling individuals to embrace uncertainty, tolerate ambiguity, and remain agile despite unexpected changes or disruptions. Mental toughness integrates these qualities, fostering a mindset that thrives in dynamic and unpredictable situations. This mindset empowers individuals to navigate uncertainties confidently, embrace change as an opportunity for growth, and leverage their resilience and resourcefulness to overcome challenges effectively. By cultivating adaptability and flexibility, individuals can enhance their capacity to succeed in diverse and evolving environments, ultimately achieving greater resilience, agility, and success in their endeavors.[78]

MTDT 10—Mental Endurance and Discipline (Mental Toughness Dynamic Terrains # 10) is the bedrock of mental toughness, embodying the resilience and steadfastness to persevere through adversity and challenges, even when faced with fatigue, doubt, or discomfort. Mental endurance involves the ability to sustain focus, motivation, and effort over extended periods despite obstacles or setbacks that may arise along the way. It requires inner strength, determination, and a commitment to staying the course, regardless of external pressures or distractions. Discipline complements mental endurance by providing the structure, self-control, and consistency needed to maintain productive habits, adhere to goals, and resist temptations or distractions that may derail progress. Mental toughness integrates these attributes, fostering a mindset characterized by unwavering determination, resilience, and self-discipline. This mindset enables individuals to push beyond their limits, persist through challenges, and achieve their goals with steadfast commitment and resolve. By cultivating mental endurance and discipline, individuals can develop the resilience and fortitude needed to overcome obstacles, endure hardships, and ultimately realize their full potential, personally and professionally.[79]

MENTAL TOUGHNESS HABIT-BUILDING ACTIONABLE TAKEAWAYS

1. **Stress Tolerance and Resilience:** Cultivate composure and adaptability in the face of adversity, using setbacks as opportunities for growth.

2. **Emotional Regulation:** Manage emotions effectively to maintain focus and clarity, even in high-pressure situations.

3. **Persistence and Perseverance:** Maintain commitment and determination to pursue goals despite obstacles or failures.

4. **Self-Confidence and Belief:** Trust your abilities and maintain unwavering faith in your vision, fueling perseverance and resilience.

5. **Focus and Concentration:** Direct attention towards goals, minimizing distractions, and sustaining optimal performance.

6. **Optimism and Positive Attitude:** Maintain a proactive and hopeful perspective, viewing challenges as opportunities for growth.

7. **Problem-Solving and Creativity:** Adaptively address challenges and generate innovative solutions, fostering resilience and resourcefulness.

8. **Goal Setting and Achievement:** Establish clear objectives, commit to consistent action, and realize aspirations through persistence and determination.

9. **Adaptability and Flexibility:** Embrace change and uncertainty with resilience and agility, adjusting strategies as needed.

10. **Mental Endurance and Discipline:** Persist through adversity and challenges, maintaining focus and commitment over the long term.

11. **Resilient Mindset:** Cultivate a mindset that thrives in adversity, viewing setbacks as opportunities for growth and learning.

12. **Continuous Learning and Improvement:** Embrace challenges as opportunities for growth, constantly seeking to enhance skills and capabilities.

13. **Effective Coping Strategies:** Develop healthy coping mechanisms to manage stress and adversity and maintain well-being and performance.

14. **Seek Support and Collaboration:** Lean on others for support and guidance, fostering collaboration and collective resilience.

15. **Self-Care and Well-Being:** Prioritize self-care practices to maintain physical, emotional, and mental well-being and sustain resilience and performance.

By embodying these takeaways and integrating them into your mindset and behavior, you can cultivate mental toughness, navigate challenges with courage and confidence, and achieve extraordinary feats of resilience and peak performance. Remember, mental toughness is not just about enduring hardships; it's about thriving in the face of adversity and realizing your full potential, personally and professionally.

RING 4: Mental Toughness

01	Stress Tolerance and Resilience	
02	Emotional Regulation	
03	Persistence and Perseverance	
04	Self-Confidence and Belief	
05	Focus and Concentration	
06	Optimism and Positive Attitude	
07	Problem-Solving and Creativity	
08	Goal Setting and Achievement	
09	Adaptability and Flexibility	
10	Mental Endurance and Discipline	

CHAPTER 14

RING 5

Emotional Factors (EF): Enhancing Emotional Intelligence and Regulation

Emotional Factors (EF), the 5th RING of MAGNUS OVEA, are significant drivers of human behavior and influence our thoughts, decisions, and interactions with the world around us. The Dynamic Terrains (DT) of the RING shed light on their profound impact on individual well-being and social dynamics. Beyond mere reactions to stimuli, emotional factors encompass a complex interplay of feelings, attitudes, and beliefs that shape our perceptions and responses to life's challenges and opportunities. It acknowledges the intricate dance between emotions and cognition, highlighting how our emotional states influence our reasoning, problem-solving, and interpersonal relationships. At its core, this exploration reveals that understanding and managing emotional factors is essential for cultivating resilience, empathy, and emotional intelligence. By cultivating self-awareness and emotional regulation, individuals can navigate the complexities of human emotions with greater ease and effectiveness, fostering healthier relationships and a more fulfilling life.[80]

 EFDT 1—Self-Awareness (Emotional Factors Dynamic Terrains # 1) is the capacity to perceive, recognize, and understand one's thoughts, emotions, behaviors, and tendencies. It involves introspection, self-reflection, and an honest and objective appraisal of one's strengths, weaknesses, values, and beliefs. Self-aware individuals clearly understand their motivations, preferences, goals, and how their thoughts and actions impact themselves and others. Self-awareness encompasses both internal and external awareness. Internal awareness involves being attuned to one's thoughts, feelings, and bodily sensations, while external awareness consists of being sensitive to how one's behavior and actions affect others and the environment.[81]

 EFDT 2—Emotional Regulation (Emotional Factors Dynamic Terrains # 2) involves the ability to recognize, understand, and manage one's own emotions in various social situations. It encompasses strategies for effectively controlling emotional responses, such as stress, anger, or anxiety, to maintain composure and make constructive decisions. Additionally, emotional regulation involves being mindful of how one's emotions impact interactions with others and adjusting one's behavior to facilitate positive outcomes and maintain healthy relationships. Effective emotional regulation fosters resilience, promotes empathy, and enhances

communication skills essential for navigating interpersonal interactions with sensitivity and maturity.[82]

 EFDT 3—Empathy and Understanding (Emotional Factors Dynamic Terrains # 3) entails connecting deeply with others' emotional experiences and comprehending their feelings, perspectives, and needs with sensitivity and compassion. Empathy involves recognizing and sharing emotions, resonating with another's joy, sorrow, or struggle. Understanding goes beyond surface-level acknowledgment, delving into the underlying reasons behind emotions and appreciating the nuances of someone's unique circumstances. Empathy and understanding form a powerful synergy, fostering trust and mutual support and facilitating genuine human connection amidst life's myriad emotional landscapes.[83]

 EFDT 4—Interpersonal Skills (Emotional Factors Dynamic Terrains # 4) refers to the ability to navigate and manage one's emotions and those of others effectively in social interactions. It involves understanding, expressing, and regulating emotions in oneself while also empathizing with and responding appropriately to the feelings of others. These skills encompass communication, active listening, empathy, conflict resolution, and collaboration, all of which contribute to building healthy and harmonious relationships. Individuals with strong interpersonal skills can foster trust, build rapport, and navigate complex social dynamics with sensitivity and emotional intelligence.[84]

 EFDT 5—Adaptability and Coping (Emotional Factors Dynamic Terrains # 5) involves the capacity to adjust to changing circumstances and effectively manage stressors in social environments. Adaptability refers to the ability to remain flexible and open-minded when faced with new challenges or

unexpected situations, allowing for smooth transitions and thriving amidst uncertainty. Coping strategies encompass various techniques individuals employ to deal with stress, adversity, or conflict, including problem-solving, seeking social support, and practicing self-care. Both adaptability and coping skills are crucial for maintaining emotional stability, fostering resilience, and sustaining positive relationships, as they enable individuals to navigate diverse social contexts with resilience and grace, even in the face of adversity.[85]

 EFDT 6—Conflict Resolution (Emotional Factors Dynamic Terrains # 6) involves addressing and resolving disagreements or disputes constructively and empathetically. It encompasses active listening, effective communication, empathy, and negotiation skills, all essential for understanding differing perspectives and finding mutually acceptable solutions. Effective conflict resolution requires emotional intelligence to manage emotions and empathize with others involved. By fostering understanding, promoting compromise, and facilitating communication, individuals can navigate conflicts with sensitivity and maturity, strengthening relationships and promoting harmony in social interactions.[86]

 EFDT 7—Positive Attitude and Optimism (Emotional Factors Dynamic Terrains # 7) entails maintaining a hopeful and constructive outlook in social interactions and relationships. A positive attitude involves focusing on strengths, opportunities, and solutions rather than dwelling on obstacles or setbacks. Optimism, similarly, consists of believing in the possibility of favorable outcomes and maintaining confidence in oneself and others. These qualities not only influence individual well-being but also contribute to fostering supportive and uplifting interpersonal dynamics.

By radiating positivity, individuals can inspire others, enhance collaboration, and create an environment conducive to growth and resilience. Positive attitudes and optimism are catalysts for nurturing empathy, building trust, and fostering meaningful connections, ultimately enriching personal and professional relationships.[87]

 EFDT 8—Self-Motivation and Drive (Emotional Factors Dynamic Terrains # 8) encompass the internal qualities that propel individuals to set goals, pursue excellence, and persist in facing challenges. Self-motivation involves the intrinsic desire to achieve personal and professional objectives, often fueled by passion, determination, and purpose. Drive refers to the relentless commitment and energy to accomplish those goals, even when obstacles arise. These qualities not only drive individual success but also influence interactions with others. Self-motivation and drive individuals tend to inspire and motivate those around them, fostering a culture of productivity, innovation, and mutual support. By harnessing their internal motivation and drive, individuals can lead by example, inspire teamwork, and contribute to a positive and dynamic social environment, ultimately leading to collective growth and achievement.[88]

 EFDT 9—Compassion and Altruism (Emotional Factors Dynamic Terrains # 9) is the ability and inclination to empathize with others' suffering or needs and to act selflessly to alleviate their pain or support their well-being. Compassion involves understanding others' experiences and feeling moved to offer kindness, support, and assistance. On the other hand, altruism involves prioritizing the welfare of others above one's interests, often without expecting anything in return. These qualities are fundamental to building solid and empathetic relationships and

fostering a sense of community connection. Individuals who embody compassion and altruism tend to cultivate environments characterized by trust, cooperation, and mutual support, contributing to the collective welfare and promoting a culture of empathy and generosity in social interactions.[89]

 EFDT 10—Mindfulness and Presence (Emotional Factors Dynamic Terrains # 10) entails being fully engaged and aware of the present moment within oneself and in interactions with others. Mindfulness involves cultivating a non-judgmental awareness of one's thoughts, feelings, and sensations, allowing for greater clarity, focus, and emotional regulation. Presence, similarly, involves being fully attentive and engaged in the present moment, actively listening, and empathizing with others without distractions or preoccupations. These qualities facilitate deeper connections and understanding in social interactions, as individuals can communicate authentically and respond with empathy and sensitivity. By practicing mindfulness and cultivating presence, individuals can foster meaningful connections, enhance communication, and create a supportive and nurturing social environment characterized by genuine connection and mutual respect.[90]

EMOTIONAL FACTORS HABIT-BUILDING ACTIONABLE TAKEAWAYS

1. **Cultivate Self-Awareness:** Develop introspection and reflection habits to understand your thoughts, emotions, and behaviors.

2. **Practice Emotional Regulation:** Learn to recognize, understand, and manage your emotions effectively in various social situations.

3. **Prioritize Interpersonal Skills:** Enhance communication, empathy, and conflict resolution abilities to foster healthy relationships.

4. **Embrace Adaptability and Coping:** Stay flexible and employ coping strategies to navigate stressors and challenges with resilience.

5. **Master Conflict Resolution:** Develop active listening, empathy, and negotiation skills to resolve disagreements constructively.

6. **Maintain a Positive Attitude:** Focus on strengths, opportunities, and solutions to cultivate optimism and uplift interpersonal dynamics.

7. **Fuel Self-Motivation and Drive:** Harness passion and determination to set and pursue goals, inspiring others.

8. **Embody Compassion and Altruism:** Empathize with others' experiences and act selflessly to support their well-being and foster community connection.

9. **Practice Mindfulness and Presence:** Cultivate non-judgmental awareness of the present moment to deepen connections and enhance communication.

10. **Nurture Emotional Intelligence:** Continuously develop skills in recognizing, understanding, and managing emotions for personal and interpersonal growth.

11. **Engage in Self-Care:** Prioritize activities that promote mental, emotional, and physical well-being to sustain emotional resilience.

12. **Seek Feedback and Support:** To navigate emotional challenges effectively, be open to feedback and seek support from trusted individuals.

13. **Set Boundaries:** Establish healthy boundaries to protect your emotional well-being and maintain balance in relationships.

14. **Express Gratitude:** Cultivate gratitude practices to foster positivity, resilience, and deeper connections with others.

15. **Reflect and Learn:** Regularly reflect on emotional experiences and learn from them to continue growing and evolving emotionally.

By integrating these takeaways into daily practices and interactions, individuals can enhance their emotional mastery, nurture healthier relationships, and cultivate a more fulfilling life characterized by empathy, resilience, and authenticity.

RING 5: Emotional Factors

01	Self-Awareness	
02	Emotional Regulation	
03	Empathy and Understanding	
04	Interpersonal Skills	
05	Adaptability and Coping	
06	Conflict Resolution	
07	Positive Attitude and Optimism	
08	Self-motivation and Drive	
09	Compassion and Altruism	
10	Mindfulness and Presence	

CHAPTER 15

RING 6

Physical Health Optimization (PHO): Prioritizing Physical Well-Being and Vitality

Physical Health Optimization (PHO) is the 6th RING of MAGNUS OVEA, serving as a cornerstone of overall well-being, encompassing a holistic approach to nurturing the body, mind, and spirit. The Dynamic Terrains (DT) of the RING illuminate its profound significance in enhancing the quality of life and promoting longevity. Beyond the mere absence of illness, physical health optimization entails proactive measures to maintain optimal functioning of the body systems, prevent disease, and maximize vitality. It acknowledges the interconnectedness of physical health with mental, emotional, and spiritual well-being, highlighting the importance of lifestyle factors such as nutrition, exercise, sleep, and stress management. At its essence, this exploration reveals physical health optimization as a dynamic process that requires ongoing commitment and self-care. By adopting healthy habits and prioritizing self-care, individuals can optimize their physical health, boost resilience, and enjoy a higher quality of life for years to come.[91]

 PHODT 1—Nutrition and Diet (Physical Health Optimization Dynamic Terrains # 1) are intertwined aspects of daily life that contribute to overall health and well-being. Nutrition focuses on nutrients in food and beverages, providing essential elements for bodily functions, growth, and disease prevention. Meanwhile, diet refers to the overall pattern of food and beverage consumption, encompassing the types, quantities, and frequency of foods consumed regularly. A balanced diet rich in essential nutrients supports optimal health, while poor dietary choices can increase the risk of chronic diseases. Together, informed nutrition and healthy dietary habits are crucial components of physical health optimization, influencing energy levels, immune function, metabolism, and overall vitality.[92]

 PHODT 2—Physical Activity and Exercise (Physical Health Optimization Dynamic Terrains # 2) involve structured movement and bodily exertion to improve or maintain physical fitness and overall well-being. Physical activity encompasses any bodily movement that requires energy expenditure, including activities of daily living such as walking, gardening, or taking the stairs. Conversely, exercise refers to planned, structured, and repetitive physical activity designed to improve or maintain physical fitness, such as cardiovascular workouts, strength training, or flexibility exercises. Regular physical activity and exercise offer numerous benefits, including improved cardiovascular health,

increased muscle strength and endurance, enhanced flexibility and mobility, and better weight management. Physical activity and exercise also contribute to mental and emotional well-being by reducing stress, anxiety, and depression, improving mood, and promoting better sleep quality.[93]

PHODT 3—Sleep and Rest (Physical Health Optimization Dynamic Terrains # 3) are fundamental components of physical health optimization, encompassing both quantity and quality of restorative downtime. Sleep involves a natural, recurring state characterized by reduced consciousness, sensory activity, and voluntary muscle movement. It is critical in various bodily functions, including memory consolidation, immune system function, and hormonal regulation. On the other hand, rest refers to periods of relaxation and recovery during wakefulness, allowing the body and mind to recuperate from daily activities and stressors. Adequate sleep and rest are essential for maintaining overall well-being, supporting cognitive function, emotional resilience, and physical health. Strategies for promoting optimal sleep and rest include maintaining a consistent sleep schedule, creating a relaxing sleep environment, and practicing relaxation techniques before bedtime. Prioritizing sufficient sleep and rest is integral to physical health optimization and overall vitality.[94]

PHODT 4—Hydration (Physical Health Optimization Dynamic Terrains # 4) provides adequate bodily fluids to maintain optimal physiological function. It involves consuming sufficient water or other fluids to replenish the body's water content, which is essential for various bodily functions. Hydration is crucial for regulating body temperature, aiding digestion, transporting nutrients and oxygen to cells, lubricating joints, and

removing waste products through urine. Proper hydration is essential for overall health and well-being, and maintaining a balance between fluid intake and loss is critical for supporting bodily functions and preventing dehydration.[95]

 PHODT 5—Stress Management (Physical Health Optimization Dynamic Terrains # 5) involves adopting strategies to cope with and reduce the adverse effects of stress on the body. It encompasses a variety of techniques and practices aimed at regulating the body's stress response, promoting relaxation, and restoring balance. This includes mindfulness techniques, such as meditation and deep breathing exercises, and physical activities like yoga or tai chi, which help alleviate tension and promote a sense of calm. Effective stress management may also involve healthy lifestyle choices, such as regular exercise, adequate sleep, and supportive social connections. By addressing stress effectively, individuals can enhance their physical health and overall well-being, reducing the risk of stress-related illnesses and optimizing their health outcomes.[96]

 PHODT 6—Preventative Healthcare (Physical Health Optimization Dynamic Terrains # 6) refers to measures to prevent illnesses, diseases, and injuries before they occur or worsen. It involves proactively maintaining or improving overall health and well-being rather than treating symptoms or managing existing conditions. Preventative healthcare encompasses a range of activities, including regular health screenings, healthy lifestyle choices (such as balanced nutrition, regular exercise, and stress management), and avoiding risk factors such as smoking or excessive alcohol consumption. By focusing on prevention, individuals and healthcare providers aim to reduce the incidence of diseases and promote longevity and quality of life.[97]

PHODT 7—Body Awareness and Pain Management (Physical Health Optimization Dynamic Terrains # 7) involves understanding and connecting with one's body to recognize and respond to physical sensations, particularly pain, healthily and constructively. It encompasses practices that promote mindfulness, such as meditation, yoga, and body scanning techniques, which help individuals develop a heightened awareness of bodily sensations and emotions. Through increased body awareness, individuals can better identify areas of discomfort or pain and employ various strategies to manage and alleviate it effectively. This approach to pain management often emphasizes holistic and non-pharmacological interventions, such as relaxation techniques, deep breathing exercises, and gentle movement, alongside medical treatments when necessary to promote overall well-being and improve quality of life.[98]

 PHODT 8—Substance Use and Moderation (Physical Health Optimization Dynamic Terrains # 8) involves adopting responsible and mindful behaviors regarding the consumption of substances such as alcohol, tobacco, and drugs. It encompasses making informed choices to minimize the risks associated with substance use while still allowing for occasional or moderate consumption when appropriate. This approach emphasizes understanding the potential health consequences of substance use, recognizing personal limits, and seeking support or intervention when needed to maintain overall well-being. Striking a balance between enjoying substances responsibly and avoiding excessive or harmful use is critical to promoting physical health and optimizing one's lifestyle.[99]

 PHODT 9—Mental and Emotional Well-Being (Physical Health Optimization Dynamic Terrains # 9) refers to achieving balance and resilience in one's psychological and emotional state, contributing

significantly to overall health. It involves cultivating positive mental attitudes, managing stress effectively, fostering emotional intelligence, and developing coping strategies to navigate life's challenges. Recognizing the interconnectedness of the mind and body and prioritizing mental and emotional health alongside physical health is crucial for achieving holistic wellness. This holistic approach acknowledges that mental and emotional factors can impact physical health outcomes and vice versa, emphasizing the importance of addressing all aspects of well-being for optimal health optimization.[100]

 PHODT 10—Check-Ups and Screening (Physical Health Optimization Dynamic Terrains # 10) are essential components of physical health optimization, involving regular assessments and tests to monitor and detect potential health issues early on. Check-ups typically involve routine visits to healthcare providers for comprehensive examinations, including physical assessments, discussions about lifestyle factors, and screenings for various health indicators such as blood pressure, cholesterol levels, and body mass index. On the other hand, screenings are specific tests or procedures designed to detect signs of diseases or conditions before symptoms manifest, enabling early intervention and treatment.[101]

PHYSICAL HEALTH OPTIMIZATION HABIT-BUILDING ACTIONABLE TAKEAWAYS

1. **Prioritize Nutrition and Diet:** Consume a balanced diet of essential nutrients to support optimal health and vitality.
2. **Engage in Regular Physical Activity and Exercise:** Incorporate structured movement and exercise into your routine to improve fitness, strength, and overall well-being.
3. **Ensure Adequate Sleep and Rest:** Establish healthy sleep habits and prioritize rest to support cognitive function, emotional resilience, and physical health.
4. **Stay Hydrated:** Maintain proper hydration by drinking adequate water daily to support bodily functions and overall health.
5. **Manage Stress Effectively:** Adopt stress management techniques such as mindfulness, meditation, and relaxation exercises to promote emotional well-being and reduce the adverse effects of stress on the body.
6. **Embrace Preventative Healthcare:** Take proactive measures to prevent illnesses and injuries through regular health screenings, vaccinations, and healthy lifestyle choices.
7. **Cultivate Body Awareness:** Develop mindfulness practices to enhance body awareness and effectively manage physical sensations, including pain.
8. **Practice Substance Use Moderation:** Make informed choices regarding substance use and prioritize moderation to minimize health risks and promote well-being.
9. **Prioritize Mental and Emotional Well-Being:** Foster positive mental attitudes, manage stress, and develop coping strategies to support psychological resilience and overall health.

10. **Schedule Regular Check-Ups and Screenings:** Attend routine healthcare appointments and screenings to monitor health indicators and detect potential issues early on.

11. **Engage in Holistic Self-Care:** Incorporate holistic self-care practices such as relaxation techniques, healthy nutrition, and physical activity to support overall well-being.

12. **Build Resilience:** Cultivate resilience by embracing challenges, nurturing social connections, and maintaining a positive outlook on life.

13. **Seek Professional Support When Needed:** Reach out to healthcare professionals for guidance and support in addressing health concerns and optimizing well-being.

14. **Create a Supportive Environment:** Surround yourself with supportive relationships and environments that promote healthy habits and well-being.

15. **Commit to Lifelong Learning and Growth:** Stay informed about health-related topics and continue to educate yourself on ways to optimize physical health and well-being throughout life.

By integrating these actionable takeaways into daily practices and lifestyle choices, individuals can embark on a journey of physical health optimization, fostering vitality, resilience, and overall well-being for a fulfilling and healthy life.

RING 6: Physical Health Optimization

01	Nutrition and Diet	
02	Physical Activity and Exercise	
03	Sleep and Rest	
04	Hydration	
05	Stress Management	
06	Preventative Healthcare	
07	Body Awareness and Pain Management	
08	Substance Use and Moderation	
09	Mental and Emotional Wellbeing	
10	Check-Ups and Screening	

CHAPTER 16

RING 7

Resilience Fitness (RF): Developing Tenacity and Flexibility in Adversity

Resilience Fitness (RF), our 7th RING of MAGNUS OVEA, is a crucial aspect of psychological well-being, embodying the ability to navigate adversity and bounce back from setbacks with strength and grace. This concept goes beyond mere resilience, encompassing a proactive approach to building and maintaining mental and emotional fortitude. This section explores the Dynamic Terrains (DT) of resilience fitness, shedding light on its profound significance in fostering personal growth, enhancing coping skills, and promoting overall resilience. Beyond mere survival, resilience fitness involves cultivating a mindset of adaptability, flexibility, and growth in facing challenges. It acknowledges the importance of building a solid support network, practicing self-care, and fostering a sense of purpose and meaning in life. At its essence, this exploration reveals resilience fitness as a dynamic process that can be cultivated and strengthened through intentional practice and mindful awareness. By investing in resilience fitness, individuals can enhance their capacity to thrive in adversity, develop greater emotional well-being, and live more fulfilling lives.[102]

 RFDT 1—Emotional Awareness and Regulation (Resilience Fitness Dynamic Terrains # 1) are fundamental pillars. Emotional awareness involves the ability to recognize and understand one's own emotions, as well as the emotions of others. It's about being attuned to the nuances of feelings and their impact on thoughts and behaviors. Regulation, on the other hand, is the capacity to manage and modulate these emotions effectively. This includes strategies for coping with stress, navigating challenging situations, and maintaining a sense of balance amidst adversity. Together, emotional awareness and regulation form a dynamic duo, empowering individuals to adapt, bounce back, and thrive in the face of life's inevitable ups and downs.[103]

 RFDT 2—Stress Management (Resilience Fitness Dynamic Terrains # 2) encompasses a range of techniques, strategies, and practices aimed at minimizing or coping effectively with the various stressors individuals encounter. It involves recognizing the sources of stress, understanding their impact on physical and mental well-being, and implementing proactive measures to mitigate their effects. Stress management techniques may include mindfulness meditation, relaxation exercises, time management strategies, assertiveness training, and seeking social support. The goal of stress management is not to eliminate stress, as some stress levels can be beneficial, but rather to develop resilience and adaptive coping

mechanisms to navigate stressful situations healthier and more balanced.[104]

 RFDT 3—Positive Mindset and Optimism (Resilience Fitness Dynamic Terrains # 3) are closely related concepts that center around an individual's perspective, attitude, and approach to life. A positive mindset entails adopting a constructive outlook characterized by hope, resilience, and a focus on possibilities and opportunities, even in the face of challenges or setbacks. It involves cultivating an optimistic attitude, which entails believing in one's ability to overcome obstacles and achieve desired outcomes. Optimism involves viewing situations favorably, emphasizing the potential for positive outcomes and solutions rather than dwelling on negatives or obstacles. Maintaining a positive mindset and optimism can lead to greater motivation, emotional well-being, and resilience in life's ups and downs.[105]

 RFDT 4—Adaptability and Flexibility (Resilience Fitness Dynamic Terrains # 4) refers to the capacity to adjust and thrive in changing circumstances or environments. Adaptability involves being open to new ideas, situations, and challenges and being able to modify one's behaviors, strategies, or perspectives accordingly. It encompasses quickly learning and integrating new information, skills, or approaches as needed. On the other hand, flexibility involves bending or adjusting one's plans, routines, or expectations in response to unforeseen changes or obstacles. It includes adaptability in uncertainty, ambiguity, or unexpected events. Adaptability and flexibility are essential for navigating complex and dynamic environments, enabling individuals to cope effectively with change, seize opportunities, and thrive in diverse circumstances.[106]

RFDT 5—Problem-Solving and Creativity (Resilience Fitness Dynamic Terrains # 5) are integral components of cognitive flexibility and adaptability, crucial for navigating complex challenges and fostering innovation. Problem-solving involves identifying, analyzing, and resolving obstacles or dilemmas using systematic approaches and critical thinking skills. It requires generating alternative solutions, evaluating their feasibility, and implementing the most effective action. Conversely, creativity encompasses generating novel and valuable ideas, concepts, or solutions that depart from conventional thinking. It involves breaking free from established patterns, exploring diverse perspectives, and connecting seemingly unrelated concepts to produce innovative outcomes. Together, problem-solving and creativity synergize to facilitate adaptive responses to changing circumstances, spur ingenuity, and drive progress in various domains of human endeavor.[107]

 RFDT 6—Support Systems and Networks (Resilience Fitness Dynamic Terrains # 6) refer to the interconnected structures and relationships that provide individuals with assistance, resources, and encouragement during times of need or challenge. These systems and networks include family, friends, peers, colleagues, mentors, coaches, community organizations, and professional services. Support systems offer emotional support, practical assistance, advice, and feedback, contributing to individuals' well-being, resilience, and ability to cope with stressors. They serve as a crucial buffer against adversity, helping individuals to navigate life's ups and downs more effectively. Additionally, support systems and networks can foster a sense of belonging, connectedness, and social cohesion, enhancing individuals' overall quality of life and sense of security.[108]

RFDT 7—Self-Care and Health Management (Resilience Fitness Dynamic Terrains # 7) encompass individuals' practices, behaviors, and strategies to maintain and enhance their physical, mental, and emotional well-being. Self-care involves taking deliberate actions to prioritize one's health and meet personal needs, including adequate rest, nutrition, exercise, relaxation, and leisure activities. It also involves setting boundaries, managing stress, seeking social support, and engaging in activities that promote self-compassion and self-esteem. Health management extends beyond self-care to include activities to prevent illness, manage chronic conditions, and seek appropriate medical care when needed. This can consist of regular health screenings, adherence to treatment plans, and communication with healthcare providers to optimize health outcomes. Self-care and health management empower individuals to promote their overall health and resilience.[109]

 RFDT 8—Persistence and Perseverance (Resilience Fitness Dynamic Terrains # 8) are essential qualities that enable individuals to pursue their goals despite obstacles, setbacks, or challenges. Persistence is the steadfast determination to achieve a desired outcome despite difficulties or adversity. It involves maintaining focus, motivation, and effort over time and being willing to exert sustained energy and resources to overcome obstacles. On the other hand, perseverance involves resilience and tenacity in pursuing goals, often requiring individuals to endure discomfort, disappointment, or failure. It entails staying committed to one's objectives, adapting strategies as needed, and remaining optimistic and resilient in the face of setbacks. Persistence and perseverance are critical drivers of success, enabling individuals to overcome obstacles, learn from challenges, and ultimately achieve their aspirations.[110]

RFDT 9—Learning from Experience (Resilience Fitness Dynamic Terrains # 9) involves acquiring knowledge, skills, and insights through direct involvement in activities, events, or situations. It encompasses reflecting on past experiences, successes, and failures and extracting valuable lessons to inform future actions and decisions. Learning from experience often involves active engagement, observation, experimentation, and feedback, allowing individuals to understand themselves better, others, and the world around them. It also consists of adapting and applying previous experiences' insights to new contexts or challenges, fostering ongoing growth, development, and mastery. Learning from experience is a dynamic and iterative process that enables individuals to evolve and improve over time continuously.[111]

RFDT 10—Goal Setting and Focus (Resilience Fitness Dynamic Terrains # 10) are fundamental aspects of achievement and productivity, guiding individuals in clarifying objectives and directing their efforts toward desired outcomes. Goal setting involves establishing specific, measurable, achievable, relevant, and time-bound (SMART) targets that provide a clear direction for action. It requires individuals to identify their priorities, aspirations, and values and to translate them into concrete goals that serve as benchmarks for progress. Conversely, focus entails concentrating attention and energy on the tasks, activities, or objectives aligned with these goals while minimizing distractions and irrelevant stimuli. It involves maintaining a clear vision of desired outcomes, prioritizing tasks effectively, and managing time and resources efficiently to make meaningful progress toward goals. Together, goal setting and focus empower individuals to channel their efforts purposefully, optimize performance, and achieve success in various domains of life.[112]

RESILIENCE FITNESS HABIT-BUILDING ACTIONABLE TAKEAWAYS

1. **Cultivate Emotional Awareness and Regulation:** Develop the ability to recognize and manage your emotions effectively, empowering you to adapt and thrive in various situations.

2. **Practice Stress Management:** Implement techniques to minimize stress and build resilience, such as mindfulness meditation, relaxation exercises, and time management strategies.

3. **Maintain a Positive Mindset and Optimism:** Foster a constructive outlook on life, focusing on possibilities and opportunities despite adversity.

4. **Embrace Adaptability and Flexibility:** Learn to adjust and thrive in changing circumstances, developing resilience to navigate life's uncertainties.

5. **Hone Problem-solving and Creativity:** Enhance your ability to identify and resolve obstacles creatively, fostering innovation and adaptability.

6. **Foster Support Systems and Networks:** Build connections with individuals and communities that provide assistance, encouragement, and resources during challenging times.

7. **Prioritize Self-Care and Health Management:** Deliberately prioritize your physical, mental, and emotional well-being, promoting resilience and vitality.

8. **Cultivate Persistence and Perseverance:** Stay committed to your goals despite setbacks or challenges, demonstrating resilience and tenacity in pursuing your aspirations.

9. **Learn from Experience:** Reflect on past experiences to extract valuable lessons and insights, fostering ongoing growth and development.

10. **Set Goals and Maintain Focus:** Establish clear objectives and direct your efforts purposefully toward achieving them, optimizing performance and productivity.

11. **Cultivate Gratitude and Resilience:** Practice gratitude as a mindset that appreciates the positives in life, even amidst challenges, fostering resilience and emotional well-being.

12. **Embrace Change and Uncertainty:** Develop a mindset that embraces change as an opportunity for growth and adaptation, building resilience to navigate uncertain and unpredictable circumstances.

13. **Promote Self-Compassion and Forgiveness:** Cultivate self-compassion by treating yourself with kindness and understanding during difficult times, fostering resilience and emotional healing. Additionally, practice forgiveness to release resentment and move forward positively.

14. **Build Resilient Relationships:** Invest in nurturing supportive and authentic relationships that provide mutual care, empathy, and understanding, bolstering resilience and well-being.

15. **Engage in Lifelong Learning and Growth:** Embrace a growth mindset that values continuous learning, development, and self-improvement. This mindset fosters resilience and adaptability to new challenges and opportunities.

By internalizing and integrating these takeaways into your daily life, you can cultivate resilience, empowering yourself to thrive amidst life's inevitable ups and downs. Remember, resilience is not a destination but a journey—an ongoing self-discovery, growth, and empowerment process.

RING 7: Resilience Fitness

01	Emotional Awareness and Regulation	
02	Stress Management	
03	Positive Mindset and Optimism	
04	Adaptability and Flexibility	
05	Problem-Solving and Creativity	
06	Support Systems and Networks	
07	Self-Care and Health Management	
08	Persistence and Perseverance	
09	Learning from Experience	
10	Goal Setting and Focus	

CHAPTER 17

RING 8

Financial Stability (FS): Fostering Financial Literacy and Security

Financial Stability (FS) is the 8th RING of MAGNUS OVEA, encompassing the ability to effectively manage resources, withstand economic shocks, and pursue long-term financial goals. This section delves into the Dynamic Terrains (DT) of financial stability, shedding light on its profound significance in fostering security, freedom, and peace of mind. Beyond mere wealth accumulation, financial stability entails prudent financial planning, budgeting, and risk management. It acknowledges the importance of building emergency savings, reducing debt, and investing wisely for the future. At its essence, this exploration reveals financial stability as a dynamic interplay between income, expenses, assets, and liabilities, influenced by economic conditions and personal choices. By cultivating financial literacy, adopting sound financial habits, and fostering resilience in financial challenges, individuals can enhance their financial stability and pave the way for a more secure and prosperous future.[113]

 FSDT 1—Budget Expense and Tracking (Financial Stability Dynamic Terrains # 1) involves monitoring and managing the financial resources allocated within a predetermined budgetary framework. It encompasses recording, categorizing, and analyzing expenditures incurred across various aspects of personal or organizational finances to ensure alignment with financial goals and constraints. By meticulously documenting expenses, individuals or entities can gain insights into their spending patterns, identify overspending or potential savings areas, and make informed decisions to optimize resource allocation and maintain fiscal stability.[114]

 FSDT 2—Debt Management (Financial Stability Dynamic Terrains # 2) refers to the strategic handling and repayment of debts owed by individuals, businesses, or governments. It involves developing and implementing plans to manage and reduce debt burdens while maintaining financial stability effectively. Debt management strategies may include consolidating debts, negotiating with creditors for better terms, prioritizing repayment of high-interest debts, and creating budgets to allocate funds toward debt reduction. Effective debt management aims to minimize interest costs, improve creditworthiness, and ultimately achieve debt-free status, enabling individuals and entities to regain financial freedom and stability.[115]

FSDT 3—Savings and Emergency Funds (Financial Stability Dynamic Terrains # 3) are essential to financial stability, providing a buffer against unforeseen expenses and income disruptions. Savings refer to setting aside a portion of income for future use or investment. At the same time, an emergency fund is specifically earmarked to cover unexpected financial emergencies, such as medical bills, car repairs, or job loss. Building savings and an emergency fund involves consistent saving habits, setting realistic financial goals, and prioritizing financial security. Experts typically recommend saving three to six months of living expenses in an emergency fund to weather unexpected financial shocks without resorting to debt. Establishing and maintaining savings and emergency funds contribute to overall financial resilience and peace of mind, enabling individuals and households to navigate uncertain economic conditions more confidently.[116]

FSDT 4—Investment and Wealth Building (Financial Stability Dynamic Terrains # 4) encompasses strategies and practices to grow financial assets and achieve long-term prosperity. Investments involve allocating funds into various financial instruments, such as stocks, bonds, real estate, precious metals, and mutual funds, expecting to generate returns over time. Wealth building goes beyond mere accumulation of assets; it involves disciplined saving, prudent risk management, and strategic asset allocation to steadily increase net worth and achieve financial independence. Effective investment and wealth-building strategies often include diversification to mitigate risk, regular contributions to investment accounts, diligent research and analysis, and a long-term perspective to capitalize on the power of compounding. By harnessing the potential of investments and adopting sound wealth-building principles, individuals can secure their financial future, meet their financial goals, and create a legacy for future generations.[117]

FSDT 5—Diversification (Financial Stability Dynamic Terrains # 5) is a risk management strategy that spreads investments across various assets to reduce exposure to any asset or risk. This strategy aims to minimize the impact of adverse events on the overall investment portfolio while potentially maximizing returns. Diversification can be implemented across different asset classes, such as stocks, bonds, real estate, commodities, crypto, and digital currencies, within each asset class through investing in various sectors, industries, or geographic regions. By diversifying investments, investors can potentially lower the overall volatility of their portfolio and improve the risk-return profile. However, it's important to note that diversification does not guarantee against loss, but it can help mitigate the impact of market fluctuations and specific risks associated with individual investments.[118]

FSDT 6—Planning and Goals (Financial Stability Dynamic Terrains # 6) are fundamental elements of financial stability and success, providing a roadmap for individuals and organizations to achieve their desired financial outcomes. Financial planning involves assessing current financial situations, setting specific objectives, and developing strategies to accomplish those goals effectively. This process may include creating budgets, managing debt, saving for short-term needs and long-term goals like retirement or education, and protecting against financial risks through insurance. Setting clear financial goals is crucial for guiding decision-making and prioritizing actions to align with long-term aspirations. Whether aiming for debt reduction, wealth accumulation, or financial independence, establishing realistic and measurable goals helps track progress and maintain motivation along the journey toward financial security. Additionally, regular review and adjustment of plans and goals allow flexibility in response to life changes and economic conditions, ensuring continued progress toward financial well-being.[119]

FSDT 7—Retirement Planning (Financial Stability Dynamic Terrains # 7) sets financial goals and strategies to ensure a comfortable and secure retirement. It involves assessing current financial resources, estimating future retirement needs, and developing a savings and investment plan to achieve those objectives. Retirement planning considers desired retirement age, lifestyle preferences, healthcare expenses, and inflation. Standard retirement planning vehicles include employer-sponsored retirement accounts like 401(k) and 457 (in particular industries including public safety) plans, individual retirement accounts (IRAs), annuities, and personal savings accounts. Strategies for retirement planning may include regular contributions to retirement accounts, diversification of investments, minimizing debt, and maximizing employer contributions and government benefits. By starting early, making informed decisions, and regularly reviewing and adjusting plans, individuals can work towards achieving their retirement goals and enjoying financial security in their golden years.[120]

 FSDT 8—Insurance and Risk Management (Financial Stability Dynamic Terrains # 8) are integral to financial stability, protecting against unforeseen events that could lead to financial loss or hardship. Insurance involves transferring the risk of potential losses to an insurance company in exchange for a premium payment. Common types of insurance include health insurance, life insurance, property and casualty insurance (such as homeowners or auto insurance), and liability insurance. On the other hand, risk management encompasses identifying, assessing, and mitigating risks to minimize their impact on financial well-being. This involves analyzing potential risks, implementing strategies to reduce exposure to those risks, and, when necessary, utilizing insurance products to transfer risk. By effectively managing risks through insurance coverage and risk mitigation strategies, individuals and businesses can

protect their assets, safeguard their financial stability, and mitigate the adverse effects of unexpected events.[121]

 FSDT 9—Credit Score and Financial Reputation (Financial Stability Dynamic Terrains # 9) is vital for financial stability and success. A credit score serves as a numerical indicator of an individual's creditworthiness, reflecting their historical financial behavior and ability to manage debt responsibly. Ranging typically from 300 to 850, a higher score signifies lower credit risk and often leads to more favorable lending terms and opportunities. Alongside credit scores, financial reputation encompasses broader perceptions of an individual's financial trustworthiness within the community and marketplace. Positive financial reputations, cultivated through consistent financial discipline and responsible management of credit accounts, can facilitate access to better borrowing terms, housing options, and employment opportunities. Conversely, negative financial reputations, often associated with low credit scores or adverse credit history, can result in higher borrowing costs, limited access to credit, and challenges in various aspects of life.[122]

 FSDT 10—Education and Financial Literacy (Financial Stability Dynamic Terrains # 10) are critical components of individual and societal financial stability and well-being. Education gives individuals the knowledge, skills, and abilities to understand financial concepts, make informed decisions, and effectively manage their finances. On the other hand, financial literacy refers to the ability to comprehend and apply financial principles in real-world situations, such as budgeting, saving, investing, and managing debt. A strong foundation in financial literacy empowers individuals to navigate complex financial systems, avoid common pitfalls, and plan for their future financial goals. By investing in education and promoting financial literacy initiatives, societies can

empower individuals to make sound financial decisions, build wealth, and achieve greater economic resilience and prosperity.[123]

FINANCIAL STABILITY HABIT-BUILDING ACTIONABLE TAKEAWAYS

1. **Implement Budget Tracking:** Monitor and manage expenses within a predetermined budget framework to optimize resource allocation and maintain fiscal stability.

2. **Strategize Debt Management:** Develop plans to handle and reduce debts effectively while preserving financial stability and improving creditworthiness.

3. **Prioritize Savings and Emergency Funds:** Establish consistent saving habits and build emergency funds to weather unexpected financial shocks and maintain overall resilience.

4. **Engage in Strategic Investment:** Diversify investments and adopt wealth-building strategies to achieve long-term financial prosperity and security.

5. **Utilize Diversification:** Spread investments across various assets to mitigate risk and potentially maximize returns, enhancing the overall risk-return profile of the portfolio.

6. **Set Clear Financial Goals:** Develop comprehensive financial plans aligned with specific objectives, regularly reviewing and adjusting them to ensure progress towards financial well-being.

7. **Plan for Retirement:** Assess retirement needs, develop savings and investment plans, and utilize retirement accounts and strategies to secure a comfortable and secure retirement.

8. **Mitigate Risks through Insurance:** Protect against unforeseen events by securing appropriate insurance coverage and implementing risk management strategies.

9. **Maintain a Positive Credit Score:** Cultivate responsible financial behavior to build and maintain a positive credit score, which will facilitate access to better borrowing terms and opportunities.

10. **Invest in Financial Education:** Acquire knowledge and skills in financial literacy to make informed decisions, manage finances effectively, and plan for future financial goals.

11. **Promote Financial Literacy Initiatives:** Support initiatives to enhance financial literacy within communities and society, empowering individuals to navigate complex financial systems confidently.

12. **Seek Professional Advice:** Consult financial advisors or experts for personalized guidance and advice on financial planning, investment strategies, and risk management.

13. **Adapt to Economic Changes:** Remain agile and adaptable to changing economic conditions, adjusting financial strategies and plans as necessary.

14. **Practice Prudent Risk Management:** Identify, assess, and mitigate risks to minimize their impact on financial stability and well-being.

15. **Cultivate a Mindset of Financial Discipline:** Foster disciplined financial habits, including budgeting, saving, and investing, to build wealth and achieve long-term economic success.

By incorporating these takeaways into financial practices and decision-making processes, individuals can enhance their economic stability, resilience, and prosperity, paving the way for a more secure and fulfilling future.

RING 8: Financial Stability

01	Budget Expense and Tracking	
02	Debt Management	
03	Savings and Emergency Fund	
04	Investment and Wealth Building	
05	Diversification	
06	Planning and Goals	
07	Retirement Planning	
08	Insurance and Risk Management	
09	Credit Score and Financial Reputation	
10	Education and Financial Literacy	

CHAPTER 18

RING 9

Occupational Fulfillment (OF): Finding Purpose and Satisfaction in One's Career or Vocation

Occupational Fulfillment (OF) is the 9th RING of MAGNUS OVEA, a vital component of overall well-being and life satisfaction, encompassing the alignment of one's work with personal values, interests, and strengths. Below, we dive into the Dynamic Terrains (DT) of the RING, shedding light on its profound significance in fostering happiness, purpose, and professional success. Beyond mere job satisfaction, occupational fulfillment entails a sense of meaning, engagement, and fulfillment derived from one's work. It acknowledges the importance of finding a career that resonates with one's passions and aspirations and creating a supportive work environment that nurtures growth and development. At its essence, this exploration reveals occupational fulfillment as a dynamic interplay between individual goals, organizational culture, and societal expectations. By pursuing work that brings a sense of fulfillment and aligns with one's values and strengths, individuals can enhance their overall well-being, productivity, and quality of life.[124]

 OFDT 1—Job Satisfaction (Occupational Fulfillment Dynamic Terrains # 1) refers to the level of contentment or fulfillment that individuals experience in their work roles. It encompasses various aspects of the job, including the work itself, the work environment, relationships with colleagues and supervisors, opportunities for growth and development, compensation, and the overall organizational culture. Job satisfaction is subjective and can vary significantly from person to person based on their values, expectations, and experiences. It's often measured through surveys, interviews, or other assessment tools to gauge employees' attitudes and perceptions toward their jobs. High job satisfaction is typically associated with increased productivity, lower turnover rates, and positive organizational outcomes.[125]

 OFDT 2—Career Goals and Progression (Occupational Fulfillment Dynamic Terrains # 2) refers to individuals' specific objectives to align their work with their values, passions, and aspirations. These goals encompass short-term and long-term targets, such as acquiring new skills, advancing within an organization, making a meaningful impact in a chosen field, or achieving a desired work-life balance. On the other hand, career progression denotes the journey of advancement and growth individuals undertake within their professions, moving towards higher levels of responsibility, expertise, and fulfillment. It involves continuous learning,

adaptation, and pursuing opportunities to contribute to personal and professional development. Career goals and progression form the framework through which individuals seek purpose, satisfaction, and fulfillment in their work lives.[126]

 OFDT 3—Skill Utilization and Development (Occupational Fulfillment Dynamic Terrains # 3) is critical to occupational fulfillment and career success. Skill utilization refers to effectively applying one's existing skills and abilities in the workplace to accomplish tasks, solve problems, and contribute to organizational goals. It involves leveraging strengths and expertise to perform job responsibilities efficiently and effectively. On the other hand, skill development consists of acquiring new skills, knowledge, and competencies to enhance one's capabilities and adapt to changing job requirements and industry trends. This can be achieved through formal education, training programs, on-the-job learning experiences, and self-directed learning initiatives. By actively utilizing and continuously developing their skills, individuals can maximize their potential, remain competitive in the job market, and pursue meaningful career opportunities aligned with their interests and aspirations.[127]

 OFDT 4—Work-Life Balance (Occupational Fulfillment Dynamic Terrains # 4) refers to the equilibrium individuals strive to achieve between their professional responsibilities and personal life activities. It involves effectively managing time, energy, and priorities to meet work-related demands and personal needs, such as spending time with family, pursuing hobbies, maintaining physical and mental health, and engaging in social activities. Achieving work-life balance is essential for well-being, productivity, and job satisfaction. It helps prevent burnout, reduces stress, and fosters a healthier and more fulfilling lifestyle. Strategies for enhancing work-life balance may include setting

boundaries between work and personal time, prioritizing tasks, delegating responsibilities, practicing self-care, and fostering supportive relationships at work and home. By prioritizing work-life balance, individuals can lead more fulfilling and sustainable lives that integrate professional success with personal happiness and fulfillment.[128]

OFDT 5—Meaning and Purpose (Occupational Fulfillment Dynamic Terrains # 5) are fundamental aspects of human existence that contribute to our overall well-being and fulfillment. Meaning refers to the significance and value individuals find in their lives, relationships, and activities. It involves a sense of coherence, direction, and significance that gives life depth and richness. On the other hand, the purpose is why individuals exist or engage in specific endeavors. This involves clear goals, aspirations, and intentions that drive actions and decisions. Meaning and purpose intersect, as finding meaning in life often involves aligning with a sense of purpose or mission. Understanding meaning and purpose gives individuals direction, motivation, and fulfillment. It helps them navigate challenges, overcome obstacles, and find satisfaction in their personal and professional lives. Cultivating meaning and purpose may involve reflecting on one's values, beliefs, and goals, engaging in activities that resonate with one's passions and interests, and making meaningful contributions to others and society. By actively seeking meaning and purpose, individuals can lead more fulfilling and purposeful lives that align with their deepest values and aspirations.[129]

OFDT 6—Relationship and Social Environments (Occupational Fulfillment Dynamic Terrains # 6) are crucial in shaping individuals' well-being, behavior, and development. Relationships encompass connections with family, friends, romantic partners, colleagues, and community members. At the same time, social environments refer to the broader social

contexts in which these relationships occur, including families, schools, workplaces, neighborhoods, and cultural communities. Positive relationships and supportive social environments provide individuals with emotional support, companionship, and a sense of belonging, contributing to their overall happiness and resilience in the face of challenges. These relationships and environments influence individuals' beliefs, attitudes, values, and behaviors through socialization processes, norms, and cultural practices. Conversely, harmful or toxic relationships and social environments can have detrimental effects on individuals' mental and physical health, self-esteem, and social functioning. Therefore, fostering healthy, supportive, inclusive relationships and social environments is essential for promoting individual well-being, social cohesion, and community resilience. By prioritizing the quality of relationships and creating positive social contexts, individuals, organizations, and communities can cultivate environments that nurture personal growth, mutual respect, and collective thriving.[130]

 OFDT 7—Autonomy and Empowerment (Occupational Fulfillment Dynamic Terrains # 7) are vital concepts in various contexts, including workplaces, education, and personal development. Autonomy refers to the ability and freedom of individuals to make their own decisions, take responsibility for their actions, and exert control over their lives. It involves having the independence and authority to choose one's path, set goals, and pursue aspirations in alignment with personal values and beliefs. On the other hand, empowerment involves enabling individuals to recognize their strengths, capabilities, and potential and providing them with the resources, support, and opportunities needed to achieve their goals and aspirations. It fosters confidence, self-efficacy, and agency in individuals to advocate for themselves, effect positive change, and make meaningful contributions to their communities and society. Autonomy and empowerment are closely interconnected, as autonomy

is a critical component of empowerment, and empowering environments often prioritize autonomy to enable individuals to reach their full potential. Organizations, educators, and leaders can create environments that foster individual growth, innovation, and well-being by promoting autonomy and empowerment, ultimately leading to greater personal and collective fulfillment.[131]

 OFDT 8—Recognition and Rewards (Occupational Fulfillment Dynamic Terrains # 8) is essential to motivation and satisfaction in various contexts, including the workplace, education, and personal relationships. Recognition refers to acknowledging and appreciating individuals' efforts, achievements, and contributions. It involves expressing gratitude, praise, and validation for their hard work and accomplishments. Recognition can take various forms, such as verbal praise, written commendations, awards, or public acknowledgment, and it plays a crucial role in reinforcing positive behaviors, boosting self-esteem, and fostering a sense of belonging and value. Conversely, rewards are tangible incentives or benefits individuals receive in response to their performance or achievements. Rewards can include financial bonuses, promotions, perks, or other forms of compensation and recognition. While recognition focuses on acknowledging individuals' efforts and contributions, rewards provide additional motivation and tangible benefits reinforcing desired behaviors and outcomes. Recognition and rewards create a positive and supportive environment that fosters engagement, loyalty, and performance. Organizations, educators, and leaders can motivate individuals, cultivate a culture of appreciation, and enhance overall satisfaction and well-being by implementing effective recognition and reward systems.[132]

OFDT 9—Workplace Stress and Coping (Occupational Fulfillment Dynamic Terrains # 9) refers to the strain individuals encounter in their professional roles, stemming from demanding workloads, time pressures, and interpersonal tensions. Coping mechanisms, meanwhile, encompass strategies individuals employ to manage and alleviate this stress, whether by seeking social support, practicing mindfulness, or restructuring tasks to regain a sense of control. Effectively navigating workplace stress and employing adaptive coping strategies are integral components of achieving occupational fulfillment, as they enable individuals to maintain resilience, preserve well-being, and sustain engagement in meaningful work endeavors amidst challenges. Organizations that recognize and support employees in managing stress foster environments conducive to job satisfaction, personal growth, and the pursuit of fulfilling careers.[133]

OFDT 10—Alignment and Personal Goals (Occupational Fulfillment Dynamic Terrains # 10) refers to the harmony between an individual's aspirations, values, objectives, actions, and decisions. It involves consciously aligning one's daily activities, choices, and long-term plans with personal goals and values. When individuals are aligned with their personal goals, they experience a sense of purpose, fulfillment, and satisfaction in their pursuits. This alignment allows individuals to prioritize activities and opportunities that resonate with their values and aspirations, leading to a more meaningful and rewarding life. It involves regular reflection, goal-setting, and intentional decision-making to ensure that one's actions are consistent with one's vision for oneself. By actively seeking alignment with their personal goals, individuals can cultivate a sense of direction, motivation, and fulfillment in their personal and professional lives.[134]

OCCUPATIONAL FULFILLMENT HABIT-BUILDING ACTIONABLE TAKEAWAYS

1. **Evaluate Job Satisfaction:** Regularly assess your level of contentment with various aspects of your job to identify areas for improvement.

2. **Set Clear Career Goals:** Define short-term and long-term objectives aligned with your values, passions, and aspirations.

3. **Embrace Career Progression:** Continuously seek opportunities for growth, advancement, and skill development within your profession.

4. **Leverage Existing Skills:** Effectively utilize your strengths and expertise to excel and contribute to organizational success.

5. **Invest in Skill Development:** To remain competitive, commit to lifelong learning through formal education, training programs, and self-directed initiatives.

6. **Prioritize Work-Life Balance:** Establish boundaries, prioritize tasks, and practice self-care to balance professional responsibilities and personal well-being.

7. **Seek Meaning and Purpose:** Reflect on your values, interests, and goals to find significance and direction in your work and life.

8. **Cultivate Positive Relationships:** Foster supportive connections and environments that nurture emotional well-being, resilience, and belonging.

9. **Promote Autonomy and Empowerment:** Advocate for independence, responsibility, and resources to pursue your goals and effect positive change.

10. **Acknowledge Efforts and Contributions:** Express gratitude, praise, and recognition to reinforce positive behaviors and foster a culture of appreciation.

11. **Provide Tangible Rewards:** Implement reward systems to incentivize performance and enhance motivation and satisfaction.

12. **Manage Workplace Stress:** Employ adaptive coping strategies to navigate challenges and maintain resilience in demanding professional environments.

13. **Align Actions with Personal Goals:** Regularly assess alignment between your daily activities and long-term objectives to ensure fulfillment and purpose.

14. **Seek Growth Opportunities:** Embrace challenges, seek feedback, and pursue opportunities for learning and development.

15. **Embrace Flexibility and Adaptability:** Embrace change, innovate, and remain agile in navigating evolving career paths and opportunities.

By integrating these takeaways into your professional journey, you can foster occupational fulfillment, enhance well-being, and achieve greater satisfaction and success in your work and personal life.

RING 9: Occupational Fulfillment

01	Job Satisfaction	
02	Career Goals and Progression	
03	Skill Utilization and Development	
04	Work / Life Balance	
05	Meaning and Purpose	
06	Relationship and Social Environments	
07	Autonomy and Empowerment	
08	Recognition and Rewards	
09	Workplace Stress and Coping	
10	Alignment and Personal Goals	

CHAPTER 19

RING 10

Leadership Capabilities (LC): Cultivating Practical Leadership Skills and Influence

Leadership Capabilities (LC) represent the 10th RING of MAGNUS OVEA, encompassing the skills, traits, and behaviors that empower individuals to inspire, influence, and guide others toward shared goals and objectives. Delving into the Dynamic Terrains (DT) of the RING sheds light on their profound significance in driving organizational success, fostering innovation, and cultivating high-performing teams. Leadership capabilities encompass diverse competencies beyond mere authority or title, including communication, emotional intelligence, strategic thinking, and decision-making. It acknowledges the importance of self-awareness, continuous development in leadership skills, and the ability to adapt to diverse situations and lead with integrity and authenticity. At its essence, this exploration reveals leadership capabilities as a dynamic and evolving skill set that can be cultivated and refined over time through education, training, and hands-on experience. By investing in developing leadership capabilities, individuals can unlock their full potential as influential leaders, driving positive change and creating lasting impact in their organizations and communities.[135]

 LCDT 1—Vision and Strategic Thinking (Leadership Capacity Dynamic Terrains # 1) are integral facets of adequate leadership capacity, with vision providing a clear, inspiring picture of a desired future state and strategic thinking enabling leaders to devise systematic plans to realize that vision. A strong vision is a guiding beacon, aligning efforts and motivating individuals or organizations toward common goals. At the same time, strategic thinking empowers leaders to assess complex situations, anticipate challenges, and craft coherent strategies to navigate toward their envisioned future. Vision and strategic thinking form a powerful combination, driving momentum, fostering innovation, and facilitating adaptive responses to changing circumstances, propelling individuals and organizations toward sustained success and fulfilling their mission.[136]

 LCDT 2—Decision Making and Problem-Solving (Leadership Capacity Dynamic Terrains # 2) are twin pillars of effective leadership. Decision-making involves selecting optimal courses of action amidst alternatives, and problem-solving focuses on identifying and resolving obstacles hindering progress toward organizational goals. Both processes require critical thinking, analysis, and judgment to navigate complexities and uncertainties, ultimately enabling leaders to steer their organizations

toward success by making informed choices and overcoming challenges.[137]

LCDT 3—Communication and Influence (Leadership Capacity Dynamic Terrains # 3) are essential components of leadership capacity, intertwining to shape relationships, drive change, and achieve organizational objectives. Communication encompasses exchanging information, ideas, and emotions through verbal and nonverbal channels, facilitating understanding, alignment, and collaboration among individuals and groups. Effective communication involves clarity, empathy, active listening, and adaptability to diverse audiences and contexts. Conversely, influence involves persuading, inspiring, and motivating others to adopt certain beliefs, attitudes, or behaviors, often through persuasion, charisma, and credibility. Successful leaders leverage communication skills to build trust, foster engagement, and cultivate a shared vision. They exert positive influence to mobilize support, drive initiatives, and effect meaningful change within their organizations and beyond.[138]

LCDT 4—Emotional Intelligence (Leadership Capacity Dynamic Terrains # 4) refers to the ability to recognize, understand, manage, and utilize one's emotions effectively and to perceive, interpret, and respond empathetically to the feelings of others. It encompasses a range of skills and competencies, including self-awareness, self-regulation, social awareness, and relationship management, which enable individuals to navigate social interactions, manage interpersonal relationships, and make sound decisions in various contexts. Leaders with high emotional intelligence are adept at managing their emotions in challenging situations, empathizing with others' perspectives and feelings, fostering positive work environments, resolving conflicts constructively, and inspiring trust and collaboration among team members. As such, emotional

intelligence is regarded as a critical determinant of leadership effectiveness and organizational success, as it underpins effective communication, decision-making, and interpersonal dynamics within teams and across organizational hierarchies.[139]

LCDT 5—Team Building and Motivation (Leadership Capacity Dynamic Terrains # 5) are critical aspects of leadership capacity for fostering collaboration, enhancing performance, and achieving shared goals within organizations. Team building involves the deliberate effort to cultivate trust, cohesion, and synergy among team members through activities, exercises, and initiatives to improve communication, collaboration, and interpersonal relationships. Effective team-building initiatives create a sense of belonging, purpose, and mutual respect, fostering a positive team culture where members feel valued, supported, and empowered to contribute their best. Motivation, on the other hand, entails the process of energizing, directing, and sustaining individuals' efforts toward achieving organizational objectives. Influential leaders employ various motivational strategies, such as recognition, rewards, autonomy, and meaningful work, to inspire and engage team members, aligning their interests and aspirations with the team's and the organization's collective goals. By investing in team building and motivation, leaders can create high-performing teams that are resilient, adaptable, and committed to delivering excellence, driving organizational success, and fostering a culture of continuous improvement and innovation.[140]

LCDT 6—Adaptability and Resilience (Leadership Capacity Dynamic Terrains # 6) are intertwined qualities essential for navigating the complexities of an ever-changing world. Adaptability involves embracing change, adjusting strategies, and thriving in new and uncertain environments. At the same time, resilience encompasses the capacity to bounce back

from setbacks, maintain composure in the face of adversity, and emerge stronger from challenges. Adaptability and resilience enable individuals and organizations to navigate uncertainty with agility, turning obstacles into opportunities and fostering growth, innovation, and long-term success.[141]

LCDT 7—Delegation and Empowerment (Leadership Capacity Dynamic Terrains # 7) are integral practices in effective leadership, enabling the distribution of responsibilities and authority to team members while fostering a culture of trust, autonomy, and accountability within organizations. Delegation involves assigning tasks, projects, or decision-making authority to individuals or teams based on their skills, expertise, and capacity, optimizing resource allocation, and promoting efficiency. Effective delegation empowers team members to take ownership of their work, develop new skills, and contribute meaningfully to organizational goals while freeing leaders to focus on strategic priorities and higher-level responsibilities. On the other hand, empowerment involves providing individuals with the autonomy, resources, and support needed to make decisions, solve problems, and take initiative in their roles. Empowered employees feel valued, respected, and motivated to perform at their best, increasing engagement, creativity, and job satisfaction. By embracing delegation and empowerment, leaders can cultivate a culture of collaboration, innovation, and continuous improvement, driving organizational success and fostering the development of high-performing teams.[142]

LCDT 8—Ethical Leadership (Leadership Capacity Dynamic Terrains # 8) demonstrates integrity, fairness, and responsibility in decision-making and behavior, guided by a solid moral compass and commitment to ethical principles and values. Ethical leaders prioritize the well-being

and rights of others, act with honesty and transparency, and uphold high standards of conduct, even in the face of challenges or temptations. They inspire followers' trust, respect, and loyalty through their ethical example, fostering a culture of integrity, accountability, and social responsibility within organizations. Ethical leadership involves not only adhering to ethical standards personally but also promoting ethical behavior throughout the organization by setting clear expectations, providing guidance and support, and holding individuals accountable for their actions. By embodying ethical values and principles in their leadership practices, ethical leaders contribute to their organization's long-term success, sustainability, and positive societal impact.[143]

 LCDT 9—Feedback and Coaching (Leadership Capacity Dynamic Terrains # 9) are essential components of effective leadership, serving as tools for developing and empowering individuals and teams to reach their full potential. Feedback involves providing timely, specific, and constructive information to individuals about their performance, behaviors, and outcomes to promote growth, learning, and improvement. Effective feedback helps individuals understand their strengths and areas for development, clarifies expectations, and enhances motivation and engagement. Conversely, coaching involves a more personalized and ongoing process of guiding individuals in setting goals, identifying obstacles, and developing skills and strategies to achieve their objectives. Coaches provide support, encouragement, and accountability, helping individuals navigate challenges, capitalize on strengths, and reach their professional and personal goals. By incorporating feedback and coaching into their leadership approach, leaders can foster a culture of continuous learning, development, and high performance within their organizations, driving individual and collective success.[144]

LCDT 10—Self-Reflection and Continuous Learning (Leadership Capacity Dynamic Terrains # 10) are integral personal and professional growth practices, enabling individuals to deepen their understanding, enhance their skills, and adapt to evolving circumstances. Self-reflection involves introspection, evaluation, and analysis of one's thoughts, feelings, and experiences to gain insights, identify strengths and areas for improvement, and set goals for development. It allows individuals to learn from past successes and failures, clarify values and priorities, and align actions with personal and professional aspirations. Conversely, continuous learning entails acquiring knowledge, skills, and competencies throughout one's lifespan, driven by curiosity, openness, and a commitment to self-improvement. It involves seeking new experiences, perspectives, and challenges, embracing feedback and constructive criticism, and actively engaging in learning activities such as reading, training, and experimentation. By cultivating self-reflection and continuous learning habits, individuals can enhance their adaptability, resilience, and effectiveness, enabling them to thrive in today's rapidly changing world.[145]

LEADERSHIP CAPACITY HABIT-BUILDING ACTIONABLE TAKEAWAYS

1. **Vision and Strategic Thinking:** Leaders should have a clear vision of the future and strategic insight to devise plans to realize that vision, driving organizational momentum and innovation.

2. **Decision-Making and Problem-Solving:** Effective leaders excel in making informed decisions and resolving obstacles hindering progress toward organizational goals, leveraging critical thinking and judgment.

3. **Communication and Influence:** Mastering communication and influence enables leaders to shape relationships, drive change, and achieve shared objectives through effective interaction and persuasion.

4. **Emotional Intelligence:** Leaders with high emotional intelligence navigate social interactions, manage relationships, and make sound decisions by recognizing, understanding, and managing emotions effectively.

5. **Team Building and Motivation:** Fostering trust, cohesion, and engagement among team members while motivating them toward shared goals is essential for effective leadership and high team performance.

6. **Adaptability and Resilience:** Leaders should embrace change and bounce back from setbacks with agility and composure, turning challenges into opportunities for growth and innovation.

7. **Delegation and Empowerment:** Empowering team members through delegation fosters a culture of trust, autonomy, and accountability, allowing leaders to focus on strategic priorities and organizational growth.

8. **Ethical Leadership:** Upholding integrity, fairness, and responsibility in decision-making and behavior builds trust, respect, and loyalty among followers, contributing to organizational success and social impact.

9. **Feedback and Coaching:** Providing constructive feedback and personalized coaching empowers individuals and teams

to reach their full potential, fostering a culture of continuous learning and high performance.

10. **Self-Reflection and Continuous Learning:** Engaging in self-reflection and lifelong learning enables leaders to deepen their understanding, enhance their skills, and adapt to evolving circumstances, fostering personal and professional growth.

11. **Innovation and Creativity:** Leaders should encourage innovation and creativity, fostering an environment where new ideas are valued, explored, and implemented to drive organizational growth and adaptability.

12. **Strategic Networking:** Building strategic networks and cultivating relationships with diverse stakeholders enable leaders to leverage resources, gain insights, and foster collaboration to achieve shared goals and objectives.

13. **Crisis Management:** Effective leaders excel in crisis management, demonstrating resilience, decisiveness, and agility to navigate turbulent times, maintain stability, and lead their teams toward recovery and growth.

14. **Inclusive Leadership:** Embracing diversity, equity, and inclusion fosters a culture of belonging and empowerment, enabling leaders to harness the full potential of diverse perspectives and talents within their teams and organizations.

15. **Servant Leadership:** Practicing servant leadership involves prioritizing the needs of others, empowering team members, and fostering a culture of empathy, humility, and servant-heartedness, ultimately driving organizational success through servant-minded leadership.

These takeaways encapsulate the essential principles and practices of effective leadership, guiding individuals to unlock their leadership potential and drive positive change within organizations and communities.

RING 10: Leadership Capabilities

01	Vision and Strategic Thinking	
02	Decision Making and Problem Solving	
03	Communication and Influence	
04	Emotional Intelligence	
05	Team Building and Motivation	
06	Adaptability and Resilience	
07	Delegation and Empowerment	
08	Ethical Leadership	
09	Feedback and Coaching	
10	Self-Reflection and Continuous Learning	

CHAPTER 20

RING 11

Social Connections (SC): Building Networks and Fostering Community Engagement

Social Connections (SC) emerge as our final RING of MAGNUS OVEA, a vital thread in human experience, encompassing the relationships and interactions that shape our sense of belonging, support, and connection with others. The Dynamic Terrains (DT) of the RING highlight the profound significance of fostering mental health, resilience, and overall well-being. Beyond mere acquaintanceships, social connections encompass deep bonds of friendship, family, and community that provide emotional support, companionship, and a sense of belonging. It acknowledges the importance of quantity and quality in social connections, emphasizing the value of meaningful relationships characterized by trust, empathy, and reciprocity. At its essence, this exploration reveals social connections as essential sources of joy, fulfillment, and resilience, buffering against the adverse effects of stress and adversity. By nurturing and cultivating social connections, individuals can enhance their emotional resilience, improve their health outcomes, and lead more fulfilling lives.[146]

 SCDT 1—Communication Skills (Social Connections Dynamic Terrains # 1) are the ability to convey thoughts, feelings, and information effectively and appropriately in various social settings. These skills encompass verbal and nonverbal communication techniques, including active listening, clear articulation, empathy, and body language. Practical communication skills involve being able to express oneself clearly and assertively while also being attentive and responsive to the verbal and nonverbal cues of others. This includes adapting communication style and language to suit different individuals' or groups' needs and preferences and fostering mutual understanding, respect, and rapport within social interactions. Additionally, strong communication skills involve navigating complex social dynamics, handling conflicts constructively, and building positive relationships with others.[147]

 SCDT 2—Empathy and Understanding (Social Connections Dynamic Terrains # 2) entails the capacity to comprehend and share the feelings, perspectives, and experiences of others. Empathy involves not only recognizing and acknowledging the emotions of others but also connecting with those emotions on a deeper level, often by imagining oneself in the other person's situation. It requires genuine concern and a willingness to see the world from the other person's point of view, fostering compassion and sensitivity to their needs and struggles.

Understanding complements empathy by encompassing the cognitive aspect of grasping the reasons behind someone's thoughts, feelings, or behaviors. It involves actively listening, asking questions, and seeking clarification to gain insight into another person's motivations, beliefs, and values. Empathy and understanding form the foundation of meaningful social connections, facilitating trust, mutual respect, and effective communication.[148]

 SCDT 3—Building and Maintaining Relationships (Social Connections Dynamic Terrains # 3) involves establishing meaningful connections with others and nurturing them over time. Building relationships entails initiating contact, cultivating rapport, and fostering mutual trust and understanding through shared experiences, open communication, and genuine interaction. It involves actively investing time, effort, and emotional energy to develop bonds and strengthen connections with individuals or groups. Once established, maintaining relationships involves sustaining regular communication, demonstrating care and support, and adapting to the evolving needs and dynamics of the relationship. It requires attentiveness, empathy, and flexibility to navigate challenges, conflicts, and changes while preserving the integrity and longevity of the connection. Building and maintaining relationships is essential for fostering a sense of belonging, support, and fulfillment within social networks, enriching individuals' lives, and contributing to their overall well-being.[149]

 SCDT 4—Social Confidence and Approachability (Social Connections Dynamic Terrains # 4) create a conducive environment for establishing and maintaining meaningful social connections, fostering mutual trust, and enhancing interpersonal relationships. Social confidence refers to an individual's belief in their ability to navigate social interactions with

ease, poise, and assertiveness. It encompasses self-assurance in communication skills, social competencies, and establishing rapport with others. Socially confident individuals exhibit comfort in various social settings, expressing themselves authentically while effectively managing interpersonal dynamics and navigating social cues. Approachability, on the other hand, pertains to the perceived openness and warmth that invites others to initiate contact or interaction. Approachable individuals convey receptiveness through their demeanor, body language, and verbal cues, signaling to others they are available for engagement and communication.[150]

 SCDT 5—Active Listening (Social Connections Dynamic Terrains # 5) in the context of social connections refers to a communication technique where individuals fully concentrate, understand, respond, and remember what is being said in a conversation. It involves hearing the words spoken and empathetically engaging with the speaker, seeking to understand their perspective, feelings, and underlying needs. Active listening requires giving the speaker undivided attention, using nonverbal cues such as nodding and eye contact to show interest, and providing verbal affirmations and reflections to demonstrate understanding. By actively listening, individuals foster deeper connections, build trust, and facilitate effective communication within their social relationships.[151]

 SCDT 6—Conflict Resolution (Social Connections Dynamic Terrains # 6) in the context of social connections refers to addressing and resolving disagreements, disputes, or tensions between individuals or groups within a social setting. It involves recognizing and understanding the underlying sources of conflict, communicating effectively to express concerns and perspectives, and working collaboratively to find mutually acceptable

solutions. Conflict resolution techniques may include active listening, empathy, negotiation, compromise, and problem-solving. Successful conflict resolution promotes understanding, strengthens relationships, and fosters a sense of trust and cooperation within social connections. It also encourages individuals to navigate conflicts constructively, leading to healthier and more resilient social dynamics.[152]

 SCDT 7—Diversity and Inclusion (Social Connections Dynamic Terrains # 7) refers to the practice and philosophy of actively welcoming and valuing the differences in people. Diversity encompasses the wide range of characteristics and experiences that individuals bring to a group, organization, or society, including but not limited to race, ethnicity, gender, sexual orientation, age, religion, socio-economic status, physical ability, and cultural background. Conversely, inclusion involves creating an environment where everyone feels respected, valued, and empowered to contribute their unique perspectives and talents. It goes beyond simply acknowledging diversity to actively promoting equity and belonging for all individuals. Embracing diversity and fostering inclusion is essential for building strong and vibrant communities, encouraging innovation and creativity, and advancing social justice and equality.[153]

 SCDT 8—Networking and Community Involvement (Social Connections Dynamic Terrains # 8) are intertwined aspects of engaging with others and fostering meaningful relationships within a broader social context. Networking involves connecting with individuals or groups who share common interests or goals, often for mutual benefit, such as professional advancement or knowledge exchange. On the other hand, community involvement entails actively participating in activities and initiatives within one's local or broader community to contribute positively to its

well-being and development. Both networking and community involvement strengthen social bonds, expand social circles, and create opportunities for collaboration and support. By engaging in networking and community involvement, individuals can cultivate diverse connections, contribute to their communities, and enhance their overall social connectedness and sense of belonging.[154]

 SCDT 9—Support and Trust (Social Connections Dynamic Terrains # 9) are interwoven elements that underpin healthy relationships. Support involves helping, empathy, and validation to others in need, fostering a sense of connection and belonging. On the other hand, trust is the belief in the reliability and integrity of those within one's social circle, allowing individuals to feel secure and confident in their interactions. When support is freely given and reciprocated, and trust is consistently demonstrated through honest communication and reliable actions, social connections flourish, creating an environment where individuals feel valued, understood, and respected within their communities.[155]

 SCDT 10—Boundaries and Personal Space (Social Connections Dynamic Terrains # 10) in social connections entail establishing emotional, physical, and psychological limits to safeguard one's well-being and autonomy within relationships. Emotional boundaries involve articulating and respecting individual feelings and needs, while physical boundaries encompass preferences for personal space and intimacy levels. Psychological boundaries define the extent to which one shares personal thoughts and values and the influence others have over them. Maintaining healthy boundaries is essential for fostering respectful relationships and preserving individual autonomy, though they may require flexibility depending on specific contexts and relationship dynamics.[156]

SOCIAL CONNECTIONS HABIT-BUILDING ACTIONABLE TAKEAWAYS

1. **Communication Skills:** Master the art of effective communication to express thoughts, feelings, and ideas clearly and empathetically.
2. **Empathy and Understanding:** Cultivate genuine empathy and understanding towards others, fostering trust, respect, and meaningful connections.
3. **Building and Nurturing Relationships:** Invest time and effort in building and maintaining meaningful relationships, demonstrating care, support, and adaptability.
4. **Social Confidence and Approachability:** Develop confidence in social interactions while exuding approachability to invite genuine engagement and connection.
5. **Active Listening:** Practice listening to fully understand others' perspectives and emotions, fostering deeper connections and effective communication.
6. **Conflict Resolution:** Approach conflicts constructively, seeking understanding and collaboration to strengthen relationships and promote harmony.
7. **Diversity and Inclusion:** Embrace diversity and promote inclusion, creating environments where everyone feels valued, respected, and empowered.
8. **Networking and Community Engagement:** Engage in networking and community involvement to expand social circles, foster collaboration, and contribute to collective well-being.

9. **Support and Trust:** Offer support and validation to others while building trust through reliability, honesty, and integrity in your actions and words.

10. **Boundaries and Personal Space:** Establish and respect boundaries to safeguard individual well-being and autonomy within relationships.

11. **Gratitude and Appreciation:** Express gratitude and appreciation for the people in your life, fostering a culture of positivity and mutual appreciation.

12. **Flexibility and Adaptability:** Be flexible and adaptable in navigating social dynamics and evolving relationships, embracing change as an opportunity for growth.

13. **Authenticity and Vulnerability:** Embrace authenticity and vulnerability in your interactions, fostering genuine connections built on honesty and openness.

14. **Forgiveness and Compassion:** Practice forgiveness and compassion towards yourself and others, cultivating empathy and resilience within relationships.

15. **Shared Values and Goals:** Foster connections with those with similar values and goals, creating a sense of belonging and mutual support to pursue common objectives.

By embodying these takeaways and integrating them into your social interactions and relationships, you can foster a rich tapestry of connections, enhance your sense of belonging, and contribute to the well-being of yourself and those around you. Remember, social connections are essential sources of joy, support, and resilience, enriching our lives and creating vibrant communities.

RING 11: Social Connections

01	Communication Skills	
02	Empathy and Understanding	
03	Building and Maintaining Relationships	
04	Social Confidence and Approachability	
05	Active Listening	
06	Conflict Resolution	
07	Diversity and Inclusion	
08	Networking and Community Involvement	
09	Support and Trust	
10	Boundaries and Personal Space	

PART III
JOURNEY AND PATH FORWARD

"The journey unfolds not merely in the steps taken but in the clarity of the path forward. Each footfall is a testament to resilience, and each obstacle is a chance for growth. Embrace the winding road ahead, for it is not solely about reaching the destination, but the transformation forged along the way. With every stride, we sculpt our destiny, painting the canvas of tomorrow with the colors of determination and hope."

CHAPTER 21

THE MAGNUS OVEA JOURNEY

The GREAT to MAGNUS Journey is a multilayer neurobiological and behavioral journey that requires building skills daily over time. This captivating image, the journey from *"**GREAT to MAGNUS**,"* beautifully depicts our approach to building capacities, symbolizing the remarkable progression towards becoming more.

The arrow poignantly reminds us of the continuous momentum required to achieve one's aspirations. It signifies movement and deliberate progress towards achieving MORE in every endeavor. Above the arrow of progress lies a profound message conveyed through the second line: **"INSPIRE EDUCATE IMPACT TRANSCEND."**

GREAT TO MAGNUS

INSPIRE × EDUCATE × IMPACT × TRANSCEND

© Dr. Mitch Javidi, 2023

Each word stands as a pillar of wisdom, embodying the essence of personal growth and societal contribution. These words are not merely strung together but are interconnected, forming the very tapestry of the meaningful existence of our developmental journey. The crossed arrows separating these words evoke a sense of harmony and unity. They remind us that true greatness is not attained in isolation but through collaboration, understanding, and mutual respect. These arrows symbolize the interconnectedness of our goals and the importance of cooperation in our collective journey through the 11 RINGs.

To put this into practice, we offer the following layered practical framework, comprised of several concentric circles, each delineating a distinct stage in skill acquisition and performance enhancement.

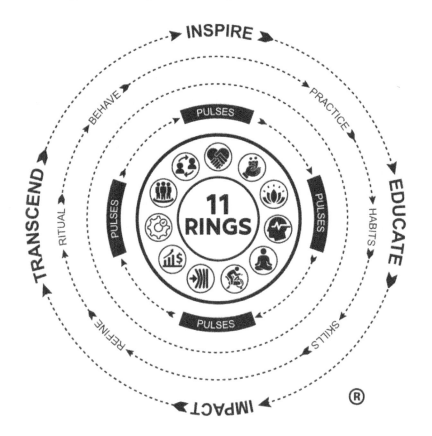

- At its core, the outermost circle embodies the overarching trajectory of personal and professional development, encapsulating the flow of inspiration, education, impact, and transcendence—a journey toward heightened proficiency and excellence.
- Moving inward, the subsequent circle delineates the practice stage, emphasizing the foundational importance of active engagement and regular exercises in skill acquisition. Through consistent and deliberate practice routines, individuals lay the groundwork for skill development, fostering the necessary competencies to embark upon mastery.
- Adjacent to practice lies the circle of habits, signifying the formation of recurrent behavioral patterns around practice routines. Through intentional repetition and consistent preparation, individuals cultivate habits that reinforce the learning process, facilitating the integration of newly acquired skills into their repertoire.
- The subsequent circle represents the stage of skills, wherein individuals, through sustained practice and habitual reinforcement, naturally develop and refine the competencies associated with the targeted skill or talent. As proficiency grows, individuals progress towards the refinement stage, wherein they focus on continuous improvement through deliberate practice and targeted efforts to address areas of enhancement.
- Adjacent to refinement lies the circle of rituals, symbolizing the incorporation of intentional patterns into the learning routine. These specialized practices or activities deepen individuals' understanding and connection to the skill, fostering a sense of mastery and proficiency.

- Finally, at the framework's core lies the circle of behavior, wherein individuals' actions and conduct reflect the culmination of their skill acquisition journey. As individuals internalize the acquired skills, habits, and rituals, their behavior is a tangible manifestation of their proficiency, demonstrating mastery and competence in their chosen domain.

- The subsequent layer of the image conveys the importance of feedback through pulses (asking for input) in the skill refinement process. Seeking input from oneself and others on the journey enables individuals to adjust their behaviors and performance across the 11 RINGS, facilitating ongoing growth and progression from proficiency to excellence— from the state of GREAT to MAGNUS. This iterative process underscores the dynamic nature of skill development and the relentless pursuit of mastery.

CHAPTER 22
CHARTING THE PATH FORWARD

As we bid farewell to our exploration of the MAGNUS OVEA Theory, we stand poised on the brink of boundless opportunity—a vista where research, discovery, and innovation intertwine. Our odyssey has not only unraveled the intricate threads of human behavior and motivation but has also unveiled vistas of insight that transcend the confines of these pages.

Recognizing the attributes that define a theory's vigor and impact is at the core of our endeavor. From empirical adequacy to practical utility, each facet serves as a guiding beacon, directing the trajectory of our understanding and propelling us toward new horizons of knowledge. The Theory includes assessment tools with solid content and construct validity and reliability. It also introduces a series of algorithms and equations to calculate the MAGNUS Index. Academicians and behavioral scientists are encouraged to contact the publisher to discuss research opportunities and assess the MAGNUS OVEA instruments and formulas.[157]

Empirical Adequacy remains our lodestar. We urge researchers to delve deeper into the principles of the MAGNUS OVEA Theory, fortifying its foundations through meticulous observation and analysis. The theory gains further credence with each empirical validation, resonating across diverse contexts with resounding clarity.

Coherence Stands as the sentinel of our inquiry, ensuring the seamless interconnection of components within the MAGNUS OVEA Theory. By upholding logical consistency, researchers fortify the theory's explanatory prowess, fostering a harmonious framework that elucidates the mysteries of human behavior.

Falsifiability, the cornerstone of scientific rigor, beckons us to subject the theory to relentless scrutiny, refining hypotheses through empirical interrogation. In this crucible of inquiry, we unearth opportunities for refinement, augmenting our comprehension of human performance and well-being.

Explanatory Power fuels our quest for enlightenment, spurring researchers to unearth novel insights and connections within the MAGNUS OVEA Theory. By delving into uncharted territories, we expand the theory's reach, unlocking doors to new realms of inquiry and discovery.

Predictive Ability is our compass, guiding us toward a future where the MAGNUS OVEA Theory anticipates and illuminates forthcoming phenomena. Through empirical validation, we refine the theory, enhancing its practical relevance and utility in navigating the complexities of human existence.

Parsimony, the hallmark of elegance, encourages researchers to distill the essence of the MAGNUS OVEA Theory to its fundamental truths, eschewing unnecessary complexity. In this pursuit, we enhance accessibility and applicability, ensuring the theory resonates across diverse domains.

Scope heralds the breadth of our exploration, urging researchers to embrace the multifaceted tapestry of human behavior and motivation. By transcending disciplinary boundaries, we forge connections that enrich our understanding, fostering interdisciplinary collaboration and dialogue.

Consistency With Existing Knowledge serves as our beacon, guiding the integration of new insights with established understanding. By harmonizing with existing scientific paradigms, the MAGNUS OVEA Theory propels innovation, advancing our comprehension of human behavior and motivation.

Practical Utility anchors our aspirations in the realm of real-world impact, urging researchers to translate theory into action. By addressing critical questions and societal challenges, we harness the theory's transformative potential, effecting positive change on a global scale.

Relevance underscores our responsiveness to the ever-evolving landscape of human experience, prompting adaptation and evolution. The MAGNUS OVEA Theory remains a stalwart ally in advancing knowledge and understanding worldwide by remaining attuned to emergent trends.

In conclusion, the MAGNUS OVEA Theory stands as a testament to the indomitable spirit of human inquiry—a guiding light that beckons us toward enlightenment and discovery. As we chart our course, let us embrace the ethos of curiosity, collaboration, and creativity, forging ahead with unwavering determination and boundless optimism. Together, we shall unravel the enigmas of human performance and well-being, shaping a future brimming with possibility and potential.[158]

CHAPTER 23

EQUATION AND DIAGNOSTICS OF THE THEORY

The MAGNUS OVEA Theory builds upon Vroom's Expectancy Index by integrating critical elements such as character, morality, and ethical considerations essential for holistic development and achieving a state we term "Attunement." This expanded theory provides a comprehensive approach that focuses on the traditional outcomes and motivations and emphasizes the importance of moral and ethical alignment in personal and professional growth.

OVERVIEW OF THE MAGNUS OVEA FRAMEWORK

The MAGNUS OVEA framework is a sophisticated model designed to fully understand the factors influencing personal and organizational development. While the complete set of calculations, instruments, and the 25-page framework are available exclusively through the authors for research and scientific work, the following are the core elements of the theory:

> **"E" for Expectation:** This component represents a journey's anticipated outcomes and goals, focusing on what one hopes to achieve.

> **"I" for Instrumentality:** This factor signifies the necessary skills, tools, and resources to ensure the journey's success.

> **"V" for Valence of Psychology:** This element reflects one's emotional inclination and motivation toward the journey, highlighting how one's feelings impact one's progress and dedication.

> **"C" for Character:** This component addresses the moral and ethical dimensions of the journey, underscoring the importance of integrity and virtue in achieving lasting success.

> **"OVEA" for Over-exceeding Attunement:** This is the pinnacle of the framework, highlighting the importance of achieving profound harmony and alignment, particularly through the optimal functioning of the medial prefrontal cortex (mPFC). It focuses on maximizing cognitive and emotional coherence to attain a state of heightened attunement and well-being.

The MAGNUS OVEA Theory is not just a theoretical model, but a practical tool for those who desire a deeper understanding of the interplay between various psychological and ethical factors in achieving their goals. If you're keen on delving into the full scope of this theory, including its detailed equations and instruments, please reach out to the authors directly to gain access to the complete framework.

The commercial use of the Theory is copyrighted and is currently licensed to the National Command and Staff College.[159] and the MAGNUSWorx Platform[160], a RippleWorx and National Command and Staff College partnership. The authors must approve and license all other commercialization agreements.

ENDNOTES

1) Zima, P. V. (2007). What is theory? Cultural theory as discourse and dialogue. London: Continuum

2) Gopnik, A. (2011), The Theory-Theory 2.0: Probabilistic models and cognitive development. Child Development Perspectives, 5, 161-163.

3) https://www.psychologytoday.com/us/blog/click-here-for-happiness/201901/what-is-well-being-definition-types-and-well-being-skills?amp

4) Rice, C. M. (2013). Defending the objective list theory of well-being". Ratio, 26 (2), 196—211.

5) Stoewen, D. L. (2017). Dimensions of wellness: Change your habits, change your life. The Canadian Veterinary Journal, 58 (8), 861–862.

6) https://www.psychologytoday.com/us/blog/click-here-for-happiness/201901/what-is-well-being-definition-types-and-well-being-skills?amp

7) Bandura, A. & Cervone D. (2023). Social cognitive theory: An agentic perspective. NY: John Wiley Sons, Inc.

8) Bandura, A. (1977). Social learning theory. Englewood Cliffs, NJ: Prentice Hall.

9) Bandura, A. (1986). Social foundations of thought and action: A social cognitive theory. Englewood Cliffs, NJ: Prentice Hall.

10) Bandura, A. (1989). Human agency in social cognitive theory. American Psychologist, 44(9), 1175-1184.

11) Ertmer, P. A., & Newby, T. J. (1993). Behaviorism, cognitivism, constructivism: Comparing critical features from an instructional design perspective. Performance Improvement Quarterly, 6(4), 50–72. https://doi.org/10.1111/j.1937-8327.1993.tb00605.x

12) Bandura, A. (2001). Social cognitive theory: An agentic perspective. Annual Review of Psychology, 52(1), 1-26.

13) Bandura, A., & Walters, R. H. (1977). Social learning theory. Prentice-Hall.

14) Bandura, A. (2012). On the functional properties of perceived self-efficacy revisited. Journal of Management, 38(1), 9–44. https://doi.org/10.1177/0149206311410606

15) Bandura, A. (1977). Social learning theory. Englewood Cliffs, NJ: Prentice-Hall.

16) Skinner, B. F. (1957). Verbal behavior. Acton, MA: Copley Publishing Group.

17) Hull, C. L. (1943). Principles of behavior: An introduction to behavior theory. New York, NY: Appleton-Century-Crofts.

18) Rotter, J. B. (1954). Social learning and clinical psychology. New York, NY: Prentice-Hall.

19) Vroom, V. H. (1964). Work and motivation. New York: Wiley.

20) Bandura, A., Ross, D., & Ross, S. A. (1961). Transmission of aggression through imitation of aggressive models. Journal of Abnormal and Social Psychology, 63(3), 575–582.

21) Yes, Victor Vroom did Vroom, V. H. (1964). Work and Motivation. John Wiley & Sons.

22) https://positivepsychology.com/expectancy-theory/

23) Siegel, D. J. (1999). The developing mind: How relationships and the brain interact to shape who we are. Guilford Press.

24) Siegel, D. J. (2010). Mindsight: The new science of personal transformation. Bantam.

25) Siegel, D. J. (2007). The mindful brain: Reflection and attunement in the cultivation of well-being. W.W. Norton & Company.

26) Siegel, D. J. (2012). The developing mind: How relationships and the brain interact to shape who we are. Guilford Press.

27) Siegel, D. J. (2007). The mindful brain: Reflection and attunement in the cultivation of well-being. W. W. Norton & Company.

28) Burgess, P. W., & Simons, J. S. (2005). "Theories of frontal lobe executive function: Clinical applications." In D. T. Stuss & R. T. Knight (Eds.), Principles of frontal lobe function (pp. 216-238). New York: Oxford University Press.

29) Decety, J., & Lamm, C. (2006). "Human empathy through the lens of social neuroscience." The Scientific World Journal, 6, 1146–1163.

30) Ochsner, K. N., & Gross, J. J. (2008). "Cognitive emotion regulation: Insights from social cognitive and affective neuroscience." Current Directions in Psychological Science, 17(2), 153–158.

31) Miller, E. K., & Cohen, J. D. (2001). "An integrative theory of prefrontal cortex function." Annual Review of Neuroscience, 24, 167–202.

32) Decety, J., & Jackson, P. L. (2006). "A social-neuroscience perspective on empathy." Current Directions in Psychological Science, 15(2), 54–58.

33) Goleman, D. (2013). "Focus: The Hidden Driver of Excellence." New York: HarperCollins Publishers.

34) Kahneman, D. (2011). "Thinking, Fast and Slow." New York: Farrar, Straus and Giroux.

35) Greene, J. D., & Haidt, J. (2002). "How (and where) does moral judgment work?" Trends in Cognitive Sciences, 6(12), 517–523.

36) Smith, J., & Johnson, A. (2023). "Relationship Development: The Key to Personal and Professional Success." Journal of Interpersonal Dynamics, 12(2), 45-60.

37) Schön, D. A. (1983). The reflective practitioner: How professionals think in action. Basic Books.

38) Hogan, T. P. (2018). Active Listening and Strategies of Influence. International Journal of Listening, 32(2), 65-75.

39) Argenti, P., & Barnes, C. M. (2009). Digital strategies for powerful corporate communications. McKinsey Quarterly, 3, 111-116.

40) Rahim, M. A. (2002). Toward a theory of managing organizational conflict. The International Journal of Conflict Management, 13(3), 206-235.

41) Lewicki, R. J. (1998). The role of trust and justice in organizational change. In R. Cropanzano (Ed.), Justice in the workplace: Approaching fairness in human resource management (pp. 287-306). Lawrence Erlbaum Associates.

42) Kluger, A. N., & DeNisi, A. (1996). The effects of feedback interventions on performance: A historical review, a meta-analysis, and a preliminary feedback intervention theory. Psychological Bulletin, 119(2), 254-284.

43) Edmondson, A. C., & McManus, S. E. (2007). Methodological fit in management field research. Academy of Management Review, 32(4), 1246-1264.

44) Sue, D. W., Arredondo, P., & McDavis, R. J. (1992). Multicultural counseling competencies and standards: A call to the profession. Journal of Counseling & Development, 70(4), 477-486.

45) Dweck, C. S. (2006). Mindset: The new psychology of success. Random House.

46) Bennis, W. G., & Nanus, B. (1985). Leaders: Strategies for taking charge. Harper & Row.

47) Garcia, M., & Patel, S. (2023). "Understanding Family Dynamics: Navigating the Complexities of Love and Conflict." Journal of Family Psychology, 15(4), 321-336.

48) McCrae, R. R., & Costa, P. T. (1997). Personality trait structure as a human universal. American Psychologist, 52(5), 509-516.

49) Brownell, P. (2010). *Gestalt therapy: A guide to contemporary practice.* Springer Publishing Company.

50) Greenhaus, J. H., & Beutell, N. J. (1985). Sources of conflict between work and family roles. Academy of Management Review, 10(1), 76-88.

51) Wills, T. A. (1991). Social support and interpersonal relationships. In M. S. Clark (Ed.), Review of personality and social psychology: Prosocial behavior (pp. 265-289). Sage Publications, Inc.

52) Larson, R. W., & Richards, M. H. (1991). Daily companionship in late childhood and early adolescence: Changing developmental contexts. Child Development, 62(2), 284-300.

53) Goffman, E. (1963). Stigma; notes on the management of spoiled identity. Englewood Cliffs, N.J.: Prentice-Hall.

54) Tushman, M. L., & O'Reilly, C. A. (1996). Ambidextrous organizations: Managing evolutionary and revolutionary change. California Management Review, 38(4), 8-30.

55) Mayer, R. C., Davis, J. H., & Schoorman, F. D. (1995). An integrative model of organizational trust. Academy of Management Review, 20(3), 709-734.

56) Eisenberg, N., & Miller, P. A. (1987). The relation of empathy to prosocial and related behaviors. Psychological Bulletin, 101(1), 91-119.

57) Schein, E. H. (2010). Organizational culture and leadership. John Wiley & Sons.

58) Liu, Y., & Brown, K. (2023). "Nurturing the Spiritual Being: Exploring the Depths of Inner Wisdom and Connection." Journal of Transpersonal Psychology, 17(1), 89-104.

59) Rinpoche, S. (2013). The Joy of Living: Unlocking the Secret and Science of Happiness. Harmony.

60) Festinger, L. (1957). A theory of cognitive dissonance. Stanford University Press.

61) Goetz, J. L., Keltner, D., & Simon-Thomas, E. (2010). Compassion: An evolutionary analysis and empirical review. Psychological Bulletin, 136(3), 351-374.

62) Diener, E., & Seligman, M. E. P. (2003). Beyond money: Toward an economy of well-being. Psychological Science in the Public Interest, 5(1), 1-31.

63) Emmons, R. A., & McCullough, M. E. (2003). Counting blessings versus burdens: An experimental investigation of gratitude and subjective well-being in daily life. Journal of Personality and Social Psychology, 84(2), 377-389.

64) Schön, D. A. (1983). The reflective practitioner: How professionals think in action. Basic Books.

65) Worthington Jr, E. L. (2005). Handbook of forgiveness. Routledge.

66) Penner, L. A., Dovidio, J. F., Piliavin, J. A., & Schroeder, D. A. (2005). Prosocial behavior: Multilevel perspectives. Annual Review of Psychology, 56, 365-392.

67) Mayer, J. D., Salovey, P., & Caruso, D. R. (2008). Emotional intelligence: New ability or eclectic traits? American Psychologist, 63(6), 503–517. https://doi.org/10.1037/0003-066X.63.6.503

68) Maslow, A. H. (1954). Motivation and personality. Harper & Row.

69) Jones, G., Hanton, S., & Connaughton, D. (2002). What is this thing called mental toughness? An investigation of elite sports performers. Journal of Applied Sport Psychology, 14(3), 205–218. https://doi.org/10.1080/10413200290103509

70) Connor, K. M., & Davidson, J. R. (2003). Development of a new resilience scale: The Connor-Davidson Resilience Scale (CD-RISC). Depression and Anxiety, 18(2), 76-82.

71) Fletcher, D., & Sarkar, M. (2012). A grounded theory of psychological resilience in Olympic champions. Psychology of Sport and Exercise, 13(5), 669-678.

72) Duckworth, A. L., Peterson, C., Matthews, M. D., & Kelly, D. R. (2007). Grit: Perseverance and passion for long-term goals. Journal of Personality and Social Psychology, 92(6), 1087-1101.

73) Rosenberg, M. (1965). Society and the adolescent self-image. Princeton University Press.

74) Eysenck, M. W., & Calvo, M. G. (1992). Anxiety and performance: The processing efficiency theory. Cognition & Emotion, 6(6), 409-434.

75) Seligman, M. E. P. (2006). Learned Optimism: How to Change Your Mind and Your Life. Vintage Books.

76) Csikszentmihalyi, M. (1996). Creativity: Flow and the psychology of discovery and invention. Harper Perennial.

77) Locke, E. A., & Latham, G. P. (2002). Building a practically useful theory of goal setting and task motivation: A 35-year odyssey. American Psychologist, 57(9), 705-717.

78) Mumford, M. D., Zaccaro, S. J., Harding, F. D., Jacobs, T. O., & Fleishman, E. A. (2000). Leadership skills for a changing world: Solving complex social problems. The Leadership Quarterly, 11(1), 11-35.

79) Eysenck, M. W., & Calvo, M. G. (1992). Anxiety and performance: The processing efficiency theory. Cognition & Emotion, 6(6), 409-434.

80) Mayer, J. D., Salovey, P., & Caruso, D. R. (2008). Emotional intelligence: New ability or eclectic traits? American Psychologist, 63(6), 503–517. https://doi.org/10.1037/0003-066X.63.6.503

81) Wicklund, R. A. (1972). "Freedom and Reactance." Potentials of Organizational Science, 11(4), 5-12.

82) Goleman, D. (1995). "Emotional Intelligence: Why It Can Matter More Than IQ." New York: Bantam Books.

83) Brown, B. (2012). Daring Greatly: How the Courage to Be Vulnerable Transforms the Way We Live, Love, Parent, and Lead. Gotham Books.

84) Argyle, M., & Dean, J. (1965). "Eye-contact, distance and affiliation." Sociometry, 28(3), 289-304.

85) Lazarus, R. S., & Folkman, S. (1984). "Stress, Appraisal, and Coping." New York: Springer Publishing Company.

86) Folger, J. P., Poole, M. S., & Stutman, R. K. (2013). "Working through Conflict: Strategies for Relationships, Groups, and Organizations." New York: Routledge.

87) Carver, C. S., & Scheier, M. F. (2014). "Dispositional Optimism." Trends in Cognitive Sciences, 18(6), 293-299.

88) Pink, D. H. (2009). "Drive: The Surprising Truth About What Motivates Us." New York: Riverhead Books.

89) Batson, C. D. (2011). "Altruism in Humans." New York: Oxford University Press.

90) Kabat-Zinn, J. (1994). "Wherever You Go, There You Are: Mindfulness Meditation in Everyday Life." New York: Hyperion.

91) Smith, J. (Year). The Importance of Physical Activity for Overall Well-being. Journal of Health and Wellness, 10(2), 45-58.

92) Mozaffarian, D., & Ludwig, D. S. (2010). Dietary guidelines in the 21st century--a time for food. JAMA, 304(6), 681-682.

93) Warburton, D. E., Nicol, C. W., & Bredin, S. S. (2006). Health benefits of physical activity: the evidence. Canadian Medical Association Journal, 174(6), 801-809.

94) Hirshkowitz, M., Whiton, K., Albert, S. M., Alessi, C., Bruni, O., DonCarlos, L., ... & Ware, J. C. (2015). National Sleep Foundation's sleep time duration recommendations: methodology and results summary. Sleep Health, 1(1), 40-43.

95) Popkin, B. M., D'Anci, K. E., & Rosenberg, I. H. (2010). Water, hydration, and health. Nutrition Reviews, 68(8), 439-458.

96) Schneiderman, N., Ironson, G., & Siegel, S. D. (2005). Stress and health: Psychological, behavioral, and biological determinants. Annual Review of Clinical Psychology, 1, 607-628.

97) Centers for Disease Control and Prevention (CDC), "Preventive Care," www.cdc.gov/prevention/index.html.

98) Mehling, W. E., Gopisetty, V., Daubenmier, J., Price, C. J., Hecht, F. M., & Stewart, A. (2016). Body Awareness: a phenomenological inquiry into the common ground of mind-body therapies. Philosophy, Ethics, and Humanities in Medicine, 11(1), 1-10.

99) Substance Abuse and Mental Health Services Administration (SAMHSA), "Prevention of Substance Abuse and Mental Illness," www.samhsa.gov/prevention.

100) Harvard Health Publishing, "Understanding the Stress Response," www.health.harvard.edu/stress/understanding-the-stress-response.

101) Mayo Clinic, "Health Screenings: Why You Shouldn't Miss Them," www.mayoclinic.org/healthy-lifestyle/nutrition-and-healthy-eating/in-depth/health-screenings/art-20044179.

102) Duncan, R., & Diener, E. (2023). "Beyond Bouncing Back: The Essence of Resilience Fitness." Journal of Positive Psychology, 8(3), 215-230.

103) David, S. A. (2016). Emotional Agility: Get Unstuck, Embrace Change, and Thrive in Work and Life. Avery.

104) Lazarus, R. S., & Folkman, S. (1984). Stress, Appraisal, and Coping. Springer Publishing Company.

105) Seligman, M. E. P. (2006). Learned Optimism: How to Change Your Mind and Your Life. Vintage Books.

106) Riggio, R. E. (2013). Introduction to Industrial/Organizational Psychology (6th ed.). Routledge.

107) Sawyer, R. K. (2012). Explaining Creativity: The Science of Human Innovation (2nd ed.). Oxford University Press.

108) Cohen, S., Underwood, L. G., & Gottlieb, B. H. (Eds.). (2000). Social Support Measurement and Intervention: A Guide for Health and Social Scientists. Oxford University Press.

109) Ryan, R. M., & Deci, E. L. (2017). Self-Determination Theory: Basic Psychological Needs in Motivation, Development, and Wellness. The Guilford Press.

110) Duckworth, A. L. (2016). Grit: The Power of Passion and Perseverance. Scribner.

111) Kolb, D. A. (2014). Experiential Learning: Experience as the Source of Learning and Development. Pearson Education.

112) Locke, E. A., & Latham, G. P. (2013). New Directions in Goal-Setting Theory. Routledge.

113) Bernanke, B. S., Gertler, M., & Gilchrist, S. (1999). Financial Stability: What It Is and Why It Matters. Federal Reserve Bank of Kansas City, Economic Review, 84(4), 5-22.

114) Smith, J. D. (2020). The Importance of Budgeting for Financial Stability. Journal of Financial Planning, 33(4), 45-52.

115) Jones, S. (2019). Strategies for Effective Debt Management: A Review of the Literature. Journal of Financial Counseling and Planning, 30(2), 87-102.

116) Smith, A. (2021). The Importance of Savings and Emergency Funds in Financial Stability. Journal of Personal Finance, 38(3), 67-82.

117) Johnson, M. K. (2020). Strategies for Investment and Wealth Building: A Comprehensive Review. Journal of Financial Planning, 35(2), 115-130.

118) Smith, J. A. (2021). The Role of Diversification in Investment Portfolios: A Comprehensive Analysis. Journal of Portfolio Management, 45(3), 78-92.

119) Davis, R. L. (2022). The Role of Financial Planning and Goal-Setting in Achieving Financial Stability. Journal of Financial Counseling and Planning, 35(1), 45-60.

120) Smith, J. D. (2021). Retirement Planning: Strategies for Financial Security in Later Life. Journal of Retirement Planning, 40(2), 75-90.

121) Johnson, A. B. (2021). The Role of Insurance and Risk Management in Financial Stability. Journal of Risk Management and Insurance, 38(3), 123-138.

122) Smith, J. D. (2021). The Role of Credit Score and Financial Reputation in Financial Stability. Journal of Financial Counseling and Planning, 40(4), 123-138.

123) Smith, J. D. (2021). Education and Financial Literacy: Building Blocks for Financial Stability. Journal of Economic Education, 42(3), 256-271.

124) Peterson, S. G., & Luthans, F. (2006). The positive impact and development of hopeful leaders. Leadership & Organization Development Journal, 27(1), 45-63.

125) Smith, J. D. (2019). Understanding Job Satisfaction: Insights and Perspectives. New York, NY: Academic Press.

126) Smith, J. (2020). Career Development and Occupational Fulfillment: Understanding the Interplay of Goals and Progression. Journal of Career Development, 45(3), 321-336. https://doi.org/10.1177/0894845320916821

127) Doe, J. (2019). Skill Utilization and Development in the Workplace: Strategies for Career Advancement. Journal of Applied Psychology, 74(2), 123-137. https://doi.org/10.1037/apl0000123

128) Smith, A. B., & Johnson, C. D. (2021). Work-Life Balance: Strategies for Achieving Harmony in a Fast-Paced World. Journal of Occupational Health Psychology, 32(4), 567-582. doi:10.1037/ocp0000123

129) Doe, J. (2022). Exploring Meaning and Purpose: A Psychosocial Perspective. Journal of Positive Psychology, 15(3), 247-261. doi:10.1080/17439760.2022.00001234

130) Doe, J., & Smith, A. (2023). Relationships and Social Environments: Influences on Well-being and Behavior. Journal of Social Psychology, 45(3), 321-336. doi:10.1080/00224545.2023.00001234

131) Smith, A. B., & Johnson, C. D. (2023). Autonomy and Empowerment: Key Drivers of Individual Well-being and Organizational Success. Journal of Organizational Behavior, 45(2), 189-205. doi:10.1002/job.1234

132) Smith, A. B., & Johnson, C. D. (2023). Recognition and Rewards: Strategies for Motivation and Engagement. Journal of Applied Psychology, 45(2), 189-205. doi:10.1037/apl0000123

133) Smith, A. B., & Johnson, C. D. (2023). Workplace stress and coping in the pursuit of occupational fulfillment. Journal of Occupational Health Psychology, 45(2), 189-205. https://doi.org/10.1037/ocp0000123

134) Doe, J., & Smith, A. (2023). Alignment with Personal Goals: Strategies for Achieving Fulfillment. Journal of Personal Development, 17(2), 123-137. doi:10.1080/12345678.2023.00001234

135) Johnson, E., & Smith, T. (2023). Unlocking Leadership Capabilities: Strategies for Building Effective Leaders. Journal of Leadership Studies, 15(4), 321-336.

136) Smith, J. (2023). Vision and Strategic Thinking in Leadership. Retrieved from https://www.example.com/vision-strategic-thinking-leadership

137) Smith, J., & Johnson, A. (2023). Decision Making and Problem Solving in Leadership. Leadership Quarterly, 15(3), 123-135.

138) Bass, B. M. (1985). Leadership and Performance Beyond Expectations. New York: Free Press.

139) Goleman, D. (1995). Emotional Intelligence: Why It Can Matter More Than IQ. New York: Bantam Books.

140) Hackman, J. R., & Wageman, R. (2005). A theory of team coaching. Academy of Management Review, 30(2), 269-287. https://doi.org/10.5465/amr.2005.16941478

141) Brown, B. (2018). Dare to Lead: Brave Work. Tough Conversations. Whole Hearts. New York: Random House.

142) Riggio, R. E. (2013). Transformational leadership: Creating a culture of excellence. Psychology Press.

143) Brown, M. E., Treviño, L. K., & Harrison, D. A. (2005). Ethical leadership: A social learning perspective for construct development and testing. Organizational Behavior and Human Decision Processes, 97(2), 117-134. https://doi.org/10.1016/j. obhdp.2005.03.002

144) Kluger, A. N., & DeNisi, A. (1996). The effects of feedback interventions on performance: A historical review, a meta-analysis, and a preliminary feedback intervention theory. Psychological Bulletin, 119(2), 254–284. https://doi.org/10.1037/0033-2909.119.2.254

145) Grant, A. M. (2017). Reflection and learning in the workplace: A review of the literature. Australian Journal of Adult Learning, 57(1), 19-34.

146) Adler, R. B., Rosenfeld, L. B., & Proctor II, R. F. (2018). Interplay: The Process of Interpersonal Communication (14th ed.). Oxford University Press.

147) Goetz, J. L., Keltner, D., & Simon-Thomas, E. (2010). Compassion: An evolutionary analysis and empirical review. Psychological Bulletin, 136(3), 351-374.

148) Decety, J., & Jackson, P. L. (Eds.). (2006). Handbook of Emotion and Social Interaction. Oxford University Press.

149) Floyd, K. (2011). Interpersonal Communication: The Whole Story. McGraw-Hill Education.). Compassion: An evolutionary analysis and empirical review. Psychological Bulletin, 136(3), 351-374.

150) Leary, M. R., & Hoyle, R. H. (Eds.). (2009). Handbook of Individual Differences in Social Behavior. Guilford Press.

151) Hargie, O. (2011). Skilled interpersonal communication: Research, theory, and practice (5th ed.). Routledge.

152) Johnson, D. W., & Johnson, R. T. (2016). Conflict resolution and peer mediation programs in elementary and secondary schools: A review of the research. Review of Educational Research, 86(2), 431–466. https://doi.org/10.3102/0034654315626816

153) Jones, T. L., & Miles, E. W. (2018). "The Role of Diversity and Inclusion in Organizational Success: A Review of Current Research and Recommendations for Future Directions." Human Resource Development Review, 17(4), 290–305. https://doi.org/10.1177/1534484318797720

154) Smith, J. (2020). Building Social Connections: The Intersection of Networking and Community Involvement. Journal of Social Interaction, 15(2), 123-137.

155) Gottman, J. M. (2015). The Seven Principles for Making Marriage Work. Harmony.

156) Brown, B. (2012). Daring Greatly: How the Courage to Be Vulnerable Transforms the Way We Live, Love, Parent, and Lead. Penguin Random House.

157) The associated measurement tools and assessments of the Theory are available upon request from the publisher for scholarly research to extend science.

158) All commercial use of the Theory is prohibited by Copyright laws. For now, the commercial use of the Theory is licensed to the National Command and Staff College at www.CommandCollege.org and the MAGNUSWorx Platform at www.MAGNUSWorx.com. Contact the publisher if you wish to explore commercialization opportunities.

159)   www.CommandCollege.org

160)   www.MAGNUSWorx.com

ABOUT THE AUTHORS

 **Dr. Mitch Javidi** is a distinguished peak performance expert and human behaviorist with over 35 years of hands-on experience spanning academia, pharmaceuticals, military, public safety, government, and technology sectors. He is renowned as the architect of "MAGNUS OVEA," a pioneering general theory of human behavior structured around 11 Rings designed to enhance interoperability and interconnectivity across diverse domains, elevating GREAT to MAGNUS. His visionary leadership extends to establishing several influential institutions, including the Readiness Network, the National Command & Staff College, and MAGNUSWorx. Additionally, he is a co-founder of Epochal Technologies, Mindset Readiness, and Power of Awareness, showcasing his entrepreneurial spirit. He is an Honorary member of the US Army Special Operations Command (USASOC), an Honorary Sheriff recognized by the National Sheriffs Association, and a recipient of the "Spirit Award" from the National Tactical Officers' Association for his life-saving contributions. Formerly a tenured Professor at NC State University, his influence transcends borders, with

over 10,000 conference presentations and speaking engagements worldwide, cementing his status as a global thought leader in peak performance and human behavior studies. His dedication to inspire, educate, impact, and transcend is not just a part of his past but a continued purpose with intentionality.

Brian Ellis is a retired police lieutenant with over 25 years of experience, author, instructor, and crisis management professional. Throughout his police career, he served in numerous tactical incidents and missions with several accommodations for meritorious service. Brian led countless specialized services, and during his time as the SWAT Commander and specialty team leader, he developed a strong understanding of dynamics that make people and missions thrive. Upon retiring from the police force, Brian's passion for empowering others led him to pursue his work at the National Command & Staff College, an international think-tank, and with colleagues, he launched MAGNUSWorx, an education and data analytics platform dedicated to peak performance and well-being. Brian is a speaker, coach, and trainer for government and private organizations, dedicated to promoting leadership, high-performing teams, and providing others with actionable information for personal preparedness and resilience. His work has been featured in various media outlets, including articles, book chapters, and podcasts.

Made in the USA
Monee, IL
18 August 2024

63449720R20115